CALMING THE CHAOS

A DRUG-FREE PROGRAM TO ELIMINATE THE SYMPTOMS OF ADHD

SANDRA STARR, ED.D.

iUNIVERSE, INC.
NEW YORK BLOOMINGTON

Calming the Chaos
A drug-free program to eliminate the symptoms of ADHD

The information, ideas, and suggestions in this book are not intended as a substitute for professional medical advice. Before following any suggestions contained in this book, you should consult your personal physician. Neither the author nor the publisher shall be liable or responsible for any loss or damage allegedly arising as a consequence of your use or application of any information or suggestions in this book.

iUniverse books may be ordered through booksellers or by contacting:

iUniverse
1663 Liberty Drive
Bloomington, IN 47403
www.iuniverse.com
1-800-Authors (1-800-288-4677)

Because of the dynamic nature of the Internet, any Web addresses or links contained in this book may have changed since publication and may no longer be valid. The views expressed in this work are solely those of the author and do not necessarily reflect the views of the publisher, and the publisher hereby disclaims any responsibility for them.

ISBN: 978-1-4401-9106-0 (sc)
ISBN: 978-1-4401-9104-6 (dj)
ISBN: 978-1-4401-9105-3 (ebk)

Printed in the United States of America

iUniverse rev. date: 11/25/2009

Acknowledgement

I wish to express my appreciation to all the parents who allowed me access to their children's medical and school records, and to all the parents and grandparents who trusted me to guide them in their quest to help their children diagnosed with ADHD. Thanks to Catherine and Pam for their editing assistance and to my friend Dianne for all her help.

DEAR READERS:

Congratulations on seeking an alternative approach to solving the dilemma associated with the ADHD diagnosis. The program that follows will help you understand and uncover the symptoms leading to the label. The vitamin regimen outlined has been shown to build strength in the immune system, and over time will eliminate the symptoms that gave rise to the label.

All parents of ADHD children and adults with ADHD deserve to know how to put an end to the relentless turmoil. You need to know that eliminating the disorder is possible through drug-free alternatives. My research proved this and currently there are hundreds of children and adults living drug-free because of this easy-to-follow program.

During my professional career, I completed a Bachelor of Arts in Medical Geography; a Masters Degree in Curriculum, the thesis of which became a published work; completed principal's qualifications; and was a member in good standing with the Ontario College of Teachers for over 40 years.

I taught elementary school for over 20 years before I accepted a promotion to vice-principal where I was responsible for school discipline. I came in direct contact with "problem" children (a high percentage of whom had ADHD) and was frustrated as to why these children misbehaved and demonstrated such inappropriate behaviour. Like so many teachers and school officials in my position, I first questioned the parenting skills, reasoning that the parents must be failing the child in some way. When I interviewed the parents, however, I most often found that they were loving and caring individuals, deeply concerned about their child's behaviour and lack of academic progress. With few exceptions, I found there were other children from the same household who did not exhibit the same behaviour or academic problems.

You may ask how I came to a different way of thinking. One evening, early in the school year, I had dinner with a friend who was a practicing dental surgeon. Over dinner she shared with me one aspect of her practice. It seemed that patients who experienced chronic headaches, fatigue, sleeping problems; mood swings, etc. had these symptoms disappear once the mercury-based fillings in their teeth were removed. This simple sharing of information led me to thinking about the children and what substances could be affecting them. When curiosity and opportunity intersect, new thinking arises and this is precisely what happened.

I resigned from my position and completed four years of research in the hope of finding answers to the bewildering behaviour of ADHD. I did this research for two reasons: one was to increase my own knowledge about the disorder so that I could better serve my students, and the other was my concern for the thousands of parents, teachers, and adults who were dealing with the problems associated with this disorder. I had also become distressed by the ever-increasing number of children being placed on medication to control the disorder.

I determined that a broader perspective had to be adopted, one that examined other factors that possibly exert a negative influence on children and adults, which causes them to exhibit anti-social behaviour and to have learning problems. This perspective encompasses a holistic philosophy, and views the body and mind as interconnected and interdependent. External factors such as environment, food, chemicals, etc. were scrutinized as possible causative factors.

I know, and have had working experience with children affected by this disorder. Since 1993 I have conducted seminars throughout Canada and the United States and have consulted with parents in Israel, England, Switzerland, Saudi Arabia, Singapore and France. It is my hope that all parents carrying the extra burden imposed by ADHD will learn about the value and success of this easy-to-follow program and allow me to guide them through the process.

My primary goal is to help all children and adults with this disorder and to provide them with the opportunity to learn how to become motivated, successful learners, to receive social acceptance, and to live drug-free.

My secondary goal is to help parents of children with ADHD and adults with ADHD realize that the guilt or shame felt, due to the resulting problems, need not be a continual burden. Many of my clients have indicated that they were made to feel responsible for their child's anti-social and inappropriate behaviour and that their approach to parenting was the cause. For the over 1000 families with whom I've worked, this couldn't be further from the truth. Every one of the parents indicated they had tried every conceivable approach recommended: parenting classes, psychotherapy, marriage counseling, medication, behaviour modification techniques, etc. with limited success. With this group of families, the majority had tried, or were still using, medication as a means of controlling the symptoms. None were content to use medication as a long-term approach and hence their interest in a drug-free alternative.

My adult clients expressed frustration revolving around failed relationships, inadequate job performance, feelings of hopelessness, depression, lethargy, etc. and when questioned about their early years, all revealed health, behaviour, and learning problems spanning most of their school years. Some, however, were able to successfully complete all of their schooling through hard work and persistence despite the fact that their IQ should have allowed them to complete the work with ease.

Since my doctoral research proved that by reducing the toxic load on the body, symptoms of ADHD were significantly reduced or entirely eliminated, and academic progress resumed, sometimes at an accelerated rate, I designed the program to help you do exactly the same thing.

In the comfort of your own home, and at your own convenience, you can become familiar with this program and begin to implement it. Through a series of questions you will come to understand which of the identified symptoms contributed to the physical, behavioural and cognitive problems.

Please remember that a journey takes time and it is completed one step at a time. The journey you are about to begin will lead you and/or your child, to a more balanced and healthful existence.

My research proved that learning and behaviour symptoms associated with ADHD disappeared by reducing the toxic load on the body. This research was conducted with 35 students in a private residential school in Ontario, Canada; all students had been labeled "ADHD" and were on various medications. Data collection included school records, medical histories, interviews and questionnaires. Data was analyzed and academic progress was reviewed and compared to former progress.

You will have success if you follow the program consistently. You may notice improvement within the first 1 to 3 months. Most clients need very little, if any, additional help once they understand the basics outlined in this book.

REMEMBER

The students in the research group only ate homemade meals, made with the freshest ingredients possible and NO JUNK FOOD was allowed. Supplementation is therefore suggested, in order to fill in nutritional gaps when a similar diet cannot be followed.

Best wishes for success on this journey,

Sandra Starr, Ed. D., (Doctor of Education)

Contents

A Personal Account

I am a mother, grandmother, educator, researcher, lecturer, and author of this book. I have been an educator for over 40 years and know the stress associated with raising and teaching children. I have used my knowledge to help thousands of children, including my own grandchildren. My two youngest grandchildren would have surely been labeled ADHD without intervention. My second granddaughter developed eczema on her arms at 9 months of age. Cortisone cream was prescribed by the doctor. Knowing from one of my clients that eczema disappeared in her daughter after following my program for 3 months, I suggested to my daughter that she could apply essential fatty acid oil to her daughter's abdominal area instead of using the cortisone. As my granddaughter grew, the eczema continued and around 2 years' of age, she started to exhibit behavioural symptoms as well. These symptoms were: violent outbursts, screaming, obstinacy, head banging, wall kicking, etc. Since she was now able to take vitamins, my daughter added a multiple vitamin to her regimen. Better behaviour was noticed at times but since the eczema was still affecting her arms, we knew that she was in much pain and discomfort. My daughter continued to give my granddaughter the essential fatty acids. As my granddaughter was now 3 years old she took the oils orally. Her arm still showed much imbalance in her system, and outbreaks were frequent, in fact, the eczema had caused the skin to lose all pigmentation. At 5 years of age she was now suffering socially as children in her senior kindergarten class made fun of her arms and frequently shunned her as if she had a contagious disease. One can only imagine how she felt. My daughter continued the vitamin and oil regimen, outlined in my book, and by 5½ my granddaughter's

1

arms were clear and the pigmentation had returned. Her behaviour was much better as was her ability to learn. She is now a competent grade 3 student and a socially behaved child. Stress however, will cause minor outbreaks. When this occurs, my daughter makes sure she gets extra rest vitamins and essential fatty acids. My younger grandson is an October-born baby. This, along with being male, indicates to all teachers that he might demonstrate some delayed learning due to immaturity. He completed JK and SK but concerns were expressed by his teachers regarding a lack of focus and poor retention of basic sight words. It was recommended that he receive daily assistance in grade 1 while waiting for testing for a learning disability most notably ADHD My daughter was pro-active and arranged for psychological testing. After the completion of the tests, the psychologist recommended that my grandson be given Ritalin™ and, if his attention improved, it would verify that he had ADHD. As an educator and mother, I was horrified at such a response. My daughter was understandably upset at the labeling but, after a 2-day deliberation, decided to stay with the vitamin and essential fatty acid regimen outlined in my program which he had been following since 2 years of age. My daughter simply increased the amounts, after consultation with a health care practitioner. It was very gratifying to all of us when the teachers called and said that my grandson "seemed to turn a corner" and was now focusing well, was completing age appropriate work and had mastered the required sight words. ALL THIS WAS ACCOMPLISHED WITHOUT THE USE OF DRUGS.

CASE HISTORIES
(STUDENT 1 IN MY RESEARCH GROUP)

Over the course of his young life, Rory, aged 10, had been labeled borderline mentally deficient, learning disabled, and ADHD. Upon examining his medical and school records I observed that he had been exposed to much medication and chemotherapy prior to birth, and had experienced much medical intervention after birth.

Rory was born 2 months prematurely, weighing just two pounds and spent the first six months of his life in the hospital. He experienced recurring respiratory problems. At 1 month of age, he had bowel surgery and at 4 months, surgery for a digestive problem. In the second month of pregnancy with Rory, his mother developed breast cancer resulting in a double mastectomy in the fifth month. From the fifth month until delivery at seven months, she received chemotherapy. From inception to 1 year of age Rory's immune and central nervous system withstood many assaults. Rory's mother continued treatment and died just prior to Rory's third birthday, contributing additional stress for him. Rory's progress was carefully monitored from birth. He received special infant and child programming from specialists at a major childrens' hospital. By the age of 4, it was apparent to specialists that he was developmentally delayed. If school officials knew of his medical history when he was admitted to school at 5 years of age, and if teachers and/or administrators took note of his prior health problems, allowances could have been made, rather than labeling him; however, in fairness to teachers, labeling was the only means of acquiring special help for him.

In grade 1 Rory experienced many learning problems. He was not ready for any academic or formal work. By the end of grade 1, he was labeled "learning disabled". Records showed that he was pre-grade one in all academic areas. Due to impulsivity, restlessness, volatile emotional state, distractibility, etc. he was independently tested, labeled ADHD and put on Ritalin™.

Rory's father and stepmother enrolled him in the private school, where my research was conducted, after spending kindergarten to Grade 3 in the public school system. During the first six months at the private school he was not able to complete any of the written assignments or tests. Over the following six months, academic gains indicated that he had now progressed to mid-grade 2 levels, a gain of one and one-half years. In his second year he again demonstrated academic improvement exceeding one year. He was now 10 years of age and functioning academically at the grade 4 levels. At this point, he was only one academic year behind. In the succeeding year he completed all requirements to achieve age-appropriate grade 5 placement. Very remarkable progress for a child previously labeled borderline mentally deficient, learning disabled and ADHD. He was now drug free and functioning well.

(STUDENT 2 IN MY RESEARCH GROUP)

Andrew was 20 years old at the time of my research at the private school. He was enrolled at the school when he was 17 years old, at which time he was functioning at an early grade 1 level in all basic skills. His functional level in comprehension and usage of verbal language was delayed but not to the same extent. Testing was impossible, given his inability to recall from short and long-term memory. When he arrived at the school, records indicated that he had the appearance of a much older man. He was slight, exhibited a curvature of the spine and was extremely withdrawn. Excerpts from academic and medical histories are as follows:

- Experienced learning problems in grade 1
- Diagnosed as hyperactive at 5 years of age and put on Ritalin at 6 years of age
- Demonstrated inappropriate behaviour
- Demonstrated poor concentration, attention span and memory recall
- Demonstrated poorly developed fine and gross motor skills, not able to print
- Spoke negatively about his ability
- Complained of constant fatigue
- Almost died at birth, frequent hospitalization
- Suffered from multiple allergies, was on many different medications
- Had operation for hernia prior to 4 years of age
- Health generally poor, frequent absences from school
- Frequently on antibiotics
- Was born prematurely, weighing under 4 pounds

By the age of 12 Andrew had received many labels and was deemed to be 6 years delayed in academic progress. He was still attempting to master counting, printing, and word recognition which is a precursor to independent reading. Within one year of registering at the private residential school, Andrew achieved 3 years' academic growth. This is extremely impressive progress for a student who had not progressed one complete year in the previous 12 years of schooling. He was also drug free, more robust in appearance and more sociable with other students, staff and visitors.

How to Use this Workbook

In order to solve a problem we must first understand it. Remember, if it is too overwhelming to implement the entire program at once, do it step by step. A suggested implementation plan is provided below, however, if something else works for you or feels more comfortable, by all means do it. The outcome should be the same - successful elimination of the symptoms most of the time.

Week 1

Read the Book —My research identified 16 common characteristics experienced by children with ADHD. Read about all of the 16 factors. I have provided examples wherever necessary. Your job will be to read, reflect, and remember what happened and make the connections. Some of you will see that your own health problems have been transferred to your son or daughter. Some of you will determine that your child's body simply suffered too many traumas. You may be amazed at what presents itself.

Begin at Factor #1 – re-read, discuss, and determine if any of this information about medication applies to you or your spouse. Keep notes. If you are an adult with ADHD, review the information with your parents. If this is not possible, or you do not wish to involve them simply move on to the next factor.

When you have finished all 16 factors go back to #1 and start counting the number of factors that you or your child endured. Some of my clients checked off 3, some 10, others have all 16 factors. The number and severity of the negative impact determines how adversely they affect the body.

Now that you know the various factors that may have contributed to the development of the disorder, you are ready to start taking action to reverse the effects.

Week 2

Find a health food store offering qualified homeopathic/naturopathic personnel.

Start taking oils and multi-vitamins. Make sure that you purchase supplements that have no dyes, preservatives, fillers, or yeast. If possible, buy whole food vitamins. These may be more expensive depending on the distributors.

Week 3

Start the elimination process

Week 4

Increase physical activity
    Note any physical or behavioural changes

Week 5

Introduce digestive enzymes and pro-biotics

Common Characteristics in ADHD Research Group of Students

This is merely a brief synopsis of what my research uncovered. I share it with you in order for you to realize any similarities in yourself or your child.

- 97% of students labeled ADHD had above-average ability
- 97% had allergies
- 68% had delayed development when learning to walk and talk
- 48% had history of allergies in immediate or extended family
- 98% had experienced behavioural problems
- 100% of the students previously on Ritalin ™ had no understanding of what had caused their problem
- 5% of the students studied had also been labeled borderline mentally retarded
- 96% of the students exhibited inconsistent learning patterns
- 80% were labeled hyperactive
- 86% had poor attendance patterns
- 75% had experienced chronic sleeping problems
- All of the students were delayed more than 2 years in academic progress

My research also revealed that these children all shared similar medical histories which give further insight into the root cause(s) of the problem. As an additional insight, I also noted that chemical pollution plays a role in causing hyperactivity and other health problems in adults and children.

16 Factors

Please remember, not all 16 factors need to be present in order for symptoms of ADHD to develop.

1. Drug use by mother or father prior to conception (or by mother during pregnancy)
   - Prescription
   - Recreational
   - Alcohol (social)
   - Smoking
2. Low birth weight/pre-term birth
3. Poverty and/or malnourishment of mother
4. Genetic predisposition to allergies
5. Exposure to toxic chemicals
6. Lead poisoning
7. Prenatal, postnatal trauma
8. Food additives/preservatives
9. Glucose intolerance
10. Adoption
11. Stress: emotional, physical, mental
12. Diet
13. Lack of exercise
14. Insufficient nutrients
15. Chemical sensitivity
16. Excessive sensory stimulation

Each factor contributes to the 'toxic load' on the body. When more factors are present, the more 'toxic' the body becomes, and the less able it is to function 'normally'. This information is intended to increase your awareness and understanding of the multiple causes of ADHD.

As you review the following factors, make notes as to which ones are applicable to you or your child. The more you examine the past, the easier it will be to make associations as to which factors contributed to the development of this disorder.

1) *DRUG USAGE BY MOTHER*

Drug usage by the mother does not always mean recreational drugs, which we know can be damaging to the developing fetus. Drug usage also includes prescription drugs, alcohol consumption, and smoking. If you did any or all of these, please try not to be hard on yourself. This information is not intended to make you feel guilty about what you have done, but rather, to increase your awareness and understanding of how various activities or habits, affect the body.

• Prescription medication and over-the-counter medication
Most of us only focus on the benefits of prescription or over-the-counter medication. Research has shown that repeated usage (particularly with antibiotics) can lead to a weakening in the body due to the development of nutritional deficiencies, or due to a reduction in the fighting ability of the 'friendly' bacteria in the intestines. 'Friendly' bacteria also assist with digestion. A reduction in their numbers (which should count in the millions), can cause food to ferment or putrefy within the intestines causing further stress on the body.

Please understand that no one factor is likely to be the cause of ADHD. It is the combination, repetition, and frequency of various factors that contribute to the weakening of one's system. If you or your spouse were on medication prior to conception, and if you had to be on medication during your pregnancy, this is a possible contributing factor to record.

Over-the-counter medication is not harmless either. Aspirin is a very commonly used drug; however, current research states that, if introduced into the market today, it would require a prescription.

- Recreational

There is substantial research indicating the probable harmful effects of these drugs on the developing fetus.

- Alcohol consumption and smoking

Since 1984, it has been known that alcohol and smoking have a negative effect on the human body. Alcohol and smoking pollute the internal environment and allow toxins to become part of the system. They also have a profound effect on nutrient absorption, the white blood cells, and the immune system. White blood cells are used to fight infections, viruses, bacteria, etc.. Alcohol consumption effectively inactivates the ability of the white blood cells anywhere from 30 minutes to 3 days, depending on the amount consumed. Since we come in contact with germs every day, it is important that our bodies have the ability to protect themselves.

If you consumed a lot of alcohol and/or smoked during your pregnancy, then your nutrient level would likely have been reduced. If your nutrients are depleted (or deficient), it is difficult to produce healthy cells for your own body and for the developing fetus. Although the fetus may have appeared to develop normally, there may have been subtle nutritional deficiencies that, when combined with other factors, give rise to certain physical symptoms.

2) LOW BIRTH WEIGHT / PRE-TERM

Low birth weight babies are frequently born earlier than expected. For this factor, low birth weight refers to those babies weighing less than four pounds. Understanding why a child is born pre-term, or with a low birth weight, is not critical, however, it is important to remember that these babies need to 'catch up' physically and developmentally.

Children born pre-term or with a low birth weight, often require extraordinary medical intervention, such as incubation, tubal feeding, operations, etc.. When infants receive so much medical intervention, they frequently require antibiotics. As previous mentioned, medication has its negative effects. In addition to the physical stress, these babies have likely also endured the emotional stress of not being with their mothers.

It is known that fluorescent lights contribute to the depletion of thiamin. Incubated babies are at risk because fluorescent lights used in incubators deplete thiamin (a B vitamin) in the body. As you become knowledgeable about the symptoms associated with various vitamin and mineral deficiencies you will be amazed at the number of common symptoms that can be traced to nutritional deficiencies.

Many of my clients remained in the hospital for the first 3 to 6 months of their lives. In fact, one of the children in my research group stayed in the hospital until he was 10 months old. Is it realistic to compare a one year old child who has had a 'normal' year, with a one year old child who has spent most of his first year in a hospital? The child, who has had a 'normal' year, will likely be able to do age-appropriate things, such as crawling, walking, interacting, and talking. The child who has been in the hospital for a length of time may have suffered many setbacks due to operations, traumas, etc.. Now let's assume both of these children are 5 years old and are ready to go to school. Do you think that the child who spent much of his/her time in the hospital is likely to be at the same developmental level as the child who has had no problems? It is highly unlikely but, unfortunately, because all of the children are chronologically the same age, they are being compared with each other. A teacher might tell the parents that their child is not advancing and learning like the others, not holding a pencil properly, not putting the square peg in the right hole, not tying his shoelaces, not speaking at an age-appropriate level, etc. It is at this juncture that the suggestion is made regarding the possibility of some kind of a learning problem.

In addition to the aforementioned problems, often pre-term and low birth weight babies have an unusual incidence of childhood diseases. These often require further treatment, leading to an increase in stress on the system, and frequently more time away from school and learning opportunities.

3) POVERTY AND/OR MALNOURISHMENT OF MOTHER (ILLNESS)

Research has shown that poverty and malnourishment of the mother present special challenges regarding the delivery of a healthy baby.

Emotional and mental stresses may additionally contribute to the body's physiological stress. It is also known that poverty in one generation produces additional problems for the next generation.

It has been speculated that approximately 95% of North Americans are malnourished. This may seem impossible because we have a seemingly abundant food supply; however, processed foods are not able to provide the proper nourishment. Processed foods provide no real nutritive value. Only natural foods can give life and promote healthy regeneration of cells. If one has some nutritional deficiency (which is likely with a processed diet) then one will likely also suffer malnourishment. Furthermore, much research suggests that illness and disease currently affecting North Americans, e.g. ear problems, gallbladder problems, colitis, etc., are due to faulty digestion.

The program outlined in this workbook will help you correct faulty digestion.

For all of you mothers, think back to when you were pregnant. Think about the various stresses placed on your body. If you are the father, think back to the condition of your health when your child was conceived. If you are an adult with ADHD talk with your parents about their health at that time. If this is not possible, think about your parents' health in general. If there were recurring infections, colds, illnesses, etc. it is probable that they had these problems as younger adults as well. Any problems (allergies, colds, infections, stresses) that you, as parents, had at the time of conception and during gestation, have the potential to cause health problems in the next generation.

Health problems or unknown nutritional deficiencies affecting the mother or father also have an effect on the developing fetus. Remember, this is not intended to make anyone feel guilty; it is aimed at increasing your awareness. I am a mother as well and was not aware of the information contained in this guidebook. Had I been aware, I certainly could have done much to prevent the problems experienced by my children.

4) GENETIC PREDISPOSITION TO ALLERGIES

If you or your spouse has allergies, the possibility exists that your child may develop or have some form of allergy because you may have transferred a weakness. An inherited weakness may not produce the same symptoms. When this is the case, we frequently don't associate our children's allergies with those experienced by ourselves.

Allergies inherently increase the toxic load and stress on the body. The body performs continuous daily functions, but when allergies are present the body suffers extra stress as it tries to get rid of the problematic substance (the toxins). The liver, kidneys, and other organs have to work harder and may also become stressed. This means that the body has less energy to do the 'everyday' tasks.

Could allergies be a possibility for your child or for yourself? Does your child (or do you) have allergies to certain foods, molds, dust, smoke, etc? Does a particular season cause problems? According to Carolee Bach, D.D., N.D., allergies can be eliminated without the use of drugs. Many of my clients tell me that their child's seasonal and food allergies disappear after following the program for 1 to 6 months. I have also been told that many children and adults no longer need asthma medication. In this area, my clients have taught me about the healing power of the body and how it can overcome its need for medication.

5) EXPOSURE TO TOXIC CHEMICALS

Exposure to toxic chemicals may not be as common as some of the other listed factors; however, there are toxic chemicals in our environment, many of which we may not be aware of. In order to fully explain this factor, here are examples from some of my clients.

CLIENT 1 was born in the Bahamas. The mother told me that when her son was a baby, it had been necessary to spray the house daily in order to control the cockroaches and other bugs. With this type of assault, the baby's system became chemically sensitive. The daily exposure to chemicals put an extra load on his liver which became "overloaded" with efforts to detoxify the rest of the body. If the liver has to detoxify too many chemicals, the excess spills back into the bloodstream and the kidneys have to do the filtering. Unfortunately, the kidneys were never meant to filter, and if they do not remove the extra toxins, the toxins continue on in the bloodstream causing more allergies or sensitivities. Whenever this boy was around any kind of chemicals, he would exhibit symptoms such as a headache, neck ache, would become obstreperous, uncooperative, etc. He became especially difficult when he was near a chlorinated swimming pool. His mother said that he became "uncontrollable".

As a teenager he loved playing sports. This is a very important activity as it helps in detoxifying the body. He was a good athlete and particularly enjoyed basketball but, whenever he entered a gym that had just been cleaned with certain chemicals, he would become obstreperous. He was kicked off the team because "he could not cooperate" and yet playing basketball was something he loved and one of the best things for him. In a situation like this, he could have been given extra Vitamin C before, and after the game and he would have been able to play more cooperatively. Vitamin C is an antioxidant, and helps to rid chemicals from the body.

All of the nutrients in the program have the ability to remove heavy metals and many of the other chemicals that you, or your child, may be exposed to on a daily basis. That is why we need to be taking supplements. We are constantly being exposed to these substances and our bodies become overwhelmed. When our bodies become overwhelmed, symptoms will appear as indicators. If there is additional stress placed on one's system, such as eating processed foods, the body does not have the opportunity to create, gain strength, and do repair. If we do not associate the symptoms with any one cause, we will continue to experience the problems associated with the symptoms. This leads to a "chronic" condition. When the body gets the nutrients it needs, the symptoms will start to disappear. It is easy to get into what I call "psychological layering". The child intends to behave in a certain way, and doesn't know why he is behaving in a different, unacceptable way. He eventually comes to believe that he must be a miserable person.

CLIENT 2 is a medical doctor who is involved in the making of prostheses. He is very chemically sensitive because he is around chemicals every day. Initially, the symptoms his body showed were headaches which he had every day. For approximately 6 months these symptoms disappeared and he thought he had just become accustomed to the substances. He actually did become 'maladapted', which means his body got used to being around the chemicals. This does not mean that he was no longer chemically sensitive. It means that his body stopped producing physical symptoms, and the problems associated with those chemicals went deeper into the body and created additional problems. He went on to say that he then started experiencing sleeping problems, but never associated them with the daily chemical exposure. If there is a problem with something in the environment, our bodies will usually produce physical symptoms first. But if we do not make the necessary adjustments (i.e. avoiding the substance or strengthening our bodies), the symptoms will change from physical symptoms to behavioural symptoms and finally produce cognitive or learning problems. When individuals are continually having difficulty concentrating, it may be that a chemical sensitivity has progressed from producing physical symptoms to cognitive ones. This client has 4 children who have all been identified as ADHD. His daily exposure to chemicals weakened his body, and these weaknesses were passed on to his children.

My clients who are dentists and nurses have also identified chemicals as problematic for their children. Why? Because dentists and nurses work with a variety of chemicals and heavy metals. One client of mine (a nurse in Nova Scotia, Canada) shared with me that every nurse who worked in her ward miscarried. They never wore gloves or masks, and they were always using heavy industrial cleaning agents in order to destroy the germs in that particular area. They were also exposed to x-rays. All of these factors combined seemed to contribute to the miscarriages. Of course, no one can be certain as to the cause or causes of these numerous miscarriages, but my client was attempting to make a logical and informed assessment of the situation. This is exactly what you need to do. Start examining your lifestyle, your diet, and your habits. Record you symptoms and start making connections. Your child's body, or your body, has been sending you signals, but without the knowledge to understand what was meant, the signals were either ignored or misinterpreted.

CLIENT 3 is a non-compliant child who is not seeing the results that he should. This particular client had been exposed to so much, that his body is very badly compromised. The following information will describe how he became so compromised.

In 1977, there was a train derailment in Mississauga, Ontario, Canada at 12 midnight and he was born at 12:10 a.m. As soon as he was born, the hospital was ordered to evacuate all patients. They took out all of the surgical patients first, and so he was in the hospital until he and his mother were evacuated at 5 or 6 a.m. At the end of that day, they were evacuated from their home as well. As we know, babies react to their environment so, in addition to the stress of the evacuation, the baby would have been inhaling pollutants and chemicals as a result of the derailment. These events would have placed further stress on his body. The intense chemical exposure for an extended period of time caused this particular child to be very chemically sensitive. He cannot go into any area where there are perfumes, sprays, air fresheners, art supplies, etc. The exposure to these chemicals produces noticeable symptoms such as, non-compliance, anti-social behaviour, and hyperactivity.

Unfortunately, he will not comply with the program and his mother is having a difficult time. He was on Ritalin™ (for ADHD) since grade 4, and Prozac™ since grade 9. When I last had contact with him, he was on probation as he had set his neighbour's house on fire. When asked by the judge why he had set the fire, he said he didn't know. It is very difficult for us to accept this response; however, if he had been exposed to chemicals, he really would not have been capable of normal thought. I am not suggesting that we excuse inappropriate behaviour; however we should understand that when people are chemically sensitive and react to these chemicals, it is similar to being under the influence of alcohol or drugs.

CLIENT 4 is a 6 year old who went into a reaction upon entering the boys' bathroom after the caretaker had just cleaned it. He had a reaction to either the deodorizer or to the cleaner used on the floors and stalls. This boy was completely out of it and had no idea where he was or what he was doing. His thought processes were not normal and because of his reaction to the chemicals, he sprayed the walls of the bathroom instead of using the urinal. He was reprimanded of course, but like the 14 year old who set his neighbour's house on fire, he did not know why he had done it.

CLIENT 5 was brought to me because he was labeled borderline mentally retarded, ADHD, and a behavioural problem. His father told me that when he cleaned his house with Pinesol™ his 9 year old son went into a rage and became completely out of control. They went on my program, were able to identify the factors, and within 3 months their child has progressed from being a non-reader, to reading at the grade 1 level. Although he was in grade 3, reading at any level was remarkable because he had not yet mastered the skill of reading. Within 6 months he was successfully completing grade 3 work, no longer had to have a teaching assistant, and no longer had the designation of "Borderline Mentally Retarded". Within this same 6-month period, his behaviour improved to such an extent that he started to have friends and the ADHD label was removed. He no longer required medication and was living drug-free for the first time since four years of age.

Around the sixth month of the program, something interesting happened. I received a phone call from his father telling me that according to the teacher the program wasn't working between 3:00 and 3:15 p.m. It did not make sense that the program failed to work only within this 15-minute time period. The teacher thought the boy was acting up because he didn't want to go home due to problems at home. His father assured me that things were actually going quite well at home so I suggested that he ask the teacher what was happening between 3:00 and 3:15. Apparently, when the children were getting ready to go home, the teacher would reward the children who had done well by stamping a "happy face" on their hands, however the ink in the stamp pad contained chemicals, and because this boy was chemically sensitive, the chemicals in the ink would go through his pores, into his bloodstream, into his brain, and he would have a reaction. I recommended that the father ask the teacher to give his son the stamp on a piece of paper. No more problems between 3:00 and 3:15. What a simple solution! I have often wished that I had known about the effects of chemicals years ago, as I could have handled situations involving my own children, and the children in my classrooms, differently.

Some of my clients experience behaviour problems only during bus rides to and from school. We have found that these behaviour problems correct themselves once the body has gained enough strength to deal with the exposure to gasoline fumes.

Think about how many of our children are being exposed to these kinds of chemicals on a daily basis, keeping them just a little bit agitated, or out of balance, preventing them from concentrating, keeping them on "the edge". Think about where you or your child could have come in contact with many chemicals. Could your child have been exposed to chemicals at a young age? Think about how your child (or you) reacts when exposed to certain smells and/or chemicals. Start thinking about what changes you can make in your home. Since the research into chemical toxicity is becoming more widespread, more non-toxic cleaning products are available.

When we reduce the toxic load on the body, the physical, behavioural, and cognitive functions will improve. Many of my clients report that rashes, headaches, general aches and pains disappear or cease.

If you or your child has a 'reaction', you can help detoxify yourself (him/her) by going out into fresh air, where possible. Take, or give your child, some Vitamin C, or a combination of antioxidants. This will reduce or eliminate the reaction. For chemically sensitive children or adults, care should be taken around chemicals that cause reactions. Remember to check with a qualified health care professional for advice.

6)   LEAD POISONING

Heavy metals such as lead, cadmium, and mercury are all around us. Our bodies have the ability to eliminate them; however, if one's body is not functioning property, the metals remain in the body and can have a phenomenally negative effect on the physical body and on the brain. Mercury fillings in the teeth can induce lethargy, mood swings, moodiness, and aches and pains. It is becoming more common to hear about dentists removing mercury fillings. They will not however, remove silver amalgam fillings (of which mercury is a part), during pregnancy.

Think of yourself or your child in terms of exposure. Did you or your child have access to lead-based paints? In houses built in the 30's, 40's and 50's lead-based paints were frequently used. Over time, the paint may have started to flake, producing lead dust particles which can cause problems when inhaled. These dust particles have been implicated in behaviour and learning problems.

A higher level of lead in your drinking or bathing water can come from lead solder on the pipes and this may cause problems. If you or your child were born before leaded gasoline was taken off the market, perhaps this exposure has contributed to the problem. Unleaded gasoline was introduced because it became apparent that leaded gas was problematic. Car and truck exhaust was known to contain lead particles. These lead particles were being absorbed by the crops near highways, and animals grazing on these crops showed elevated lead levels in their body tissue. Since many of us consume animal protein, we ultimately ingest the lead as well.

> The different types of supplements in this program contribute by helping the body remove the different kinds of metals such as, mercury, lead and cadmium.

7)   *PRENATAL, POSTNATAL TRAUMA*

If you are an adult with ADHD try to obtain this information from family members. If you are not able to have access to that information, review this section and move on to the next factor.

Prenatal trauma can be any number of events that would adversely affect mother and child. Think back to all of the things that were happening during the pregnancy to determine the kind and number of stresses on the mother's body during this time. Did the mother fall down a flight of stairs? Was she in a car accident? Did she experience a phenomenal amount of physical, emotional or mental stress during the pregnancy? Was she ill while pregnant? Was she taking antibiotics or other prescription medications? Did the family move into a new house or were renovations being done in the home during the pregnancy?

One of my clients was not able to eat anything other than tea and toast, throughout her pregnancy. She was also on medication. We know that tea and toast are not going to provide many, if any, nutrients and drinking black tea can result in a thiamin (vitamin B) deficiency. Difficult or prolonged deliveries have also been noted in the profiles of many of my clients. Physical and emotional stress places an extra burden on the body, and may lead to a deficiency in B vitamins.

Babies born with the use of forceps may have their necks slightly misaligned which contributes to faulty digestion. If there are digestive problems, it is not possible to have optimum nutrition as the body is not able to properly digest or absorb the available nutrients. There is an abundance of research illustrating the benefits of incorporating chiropractic treatment into one's life, so you may find it helpful to consult with a chiropractor.

Postnatal trauma is any event that occurred during the first several months after birth. Did your child require or experience any or many of the following: operations, antibiotics, hospital stays, convulsions, high fevers, at an early age? All of the aforementioned situations produce much stress, which is known to reduce nutrient levels in the body.

As I told you earlier, one of the children in my research group had a lot of stress at a very young age. Two months into gestation, his mother found out that she had cancer in both breasts. She was advised to abort the fetus, but she refused to do so. At five months, she had a double mastectomy and started on chemotherapy and radiation. Think of the anesthetics, the antibiotics, and the stress that she was under and now think of all that stress and its affect on her growing child. Anything that went into her body also went into the baby's body. Her baby was born pre-term and weighed only 2 pounds. Within his first month he had bowel surgery; in his fourth month he had an operation for a digestive problem; at eleven months he contracted meningitis and during this whole time he was hospitalized. During his hospital stay, it was occasionally necessary to feed him through a tube. Chemicals may be pulled from the plastic feeding tube and end up being mixed together with the liquid, and these chemicals can place additional stress on the body. At 1 year of age, he was sent home. At 3 years of age his mother died.

At 5 years of age, he started kindergarten and it was noticed that he was not able to master the same skills as the other children such as holding a pencil properly. Sometimes, this is due to a B vitamin deficiency, where the nerve bundles are not properly nourished. This makes it difficult to control a pencil or scissors properly, to catch a ball, etc. It makes it difficult to do all of those things that one 'normally' starts developing around this time. Since he was not able to make the same kind of progress as other children, testing was done and it was determined that he was learning disabled. In grade 1, he was tested again and labeled "Borderline Mentally Retarded", due to the testing results. He was also becoming more hyperactive and was additionally labeled ADHD. In addition; the school felt he was a behaviour problem. When the toxic load on his body was reduced and his body gained strength, all of the symptoms and problems disappeared.

8) *FOOD ADDITIVES/PRESERVATIVES*

More detailed information about additives and preservatives will be found later in this workbook. One of my clients said that she only had to remove BHA and BTA from her child's diet, and she no longer had a hyperactive child. BHA and BTA are preservatives that should be identified on package labels; however package labels do not always list all of the ingredients. If you cannot pronounce one of the ingredients, then a good rule to follow is "don't purchase it". It will be less expensive for you, and it will be better for your child when you eliminate the foods that have really extensive food labels. It is important to get rid of the preservatives and additives from our child's and our own diet as best we can. The research on additives and preservatives has been know since the 1970's Finegold (UCLA) concluded that certain children have a profound reaction when exposed to dyes, or certain kinds of preservatives. Prescription, over-the-counter medication, and some vitamin supplements have been found to contain dyes and preservatives.

Even though preservatives are allowed in the food we buy, this does not make them safe for us. For example, many people do not think of NutraSweet™ as being harmful, but, this substance is made from tar derivatives. Entering the body, with a molecular structure so different from a natural source of sugar, the body does not know how to break it down. Stop purchasing products that contain these harmful substances. Sugar-free gum is a commonly purchased product made with synthetic sweeteners. Stop chewing gum. If you initially find it difficult, at least reduce the amount.

Most of us have been conditioned to accept information without question, especially if the information is widely dispersed throughout our population. False information is in the marketplace, however, and because of the busy lives we lead, some items may seem desirable since they make our lives a bit easier. It becomes increasingly necessary for us to question what we put into our bodies. With the help of this workbook, it will be easier to think about substitutions and about the changes you must make.

Dyes, preservatives, and additives should be removed from our diets. The U.S. and the British governments have outlawed yellow and red dyes in foodstuffs, because of the negative implications associated with general health and children's behaviour. No one is suggesting that dyes cause hyperactivity or specific diseases, because there are many factors contributig to ADHD and other disorders. It is the combination of a number of problematic substances that can, over time, weaken the body and produce undesirable symptoms. Some people are able to 'handle' more than others and, therefore, not everyone in a family will have ADHD even if there is a genetic predisposition to it. Our bodies, and the bodies of our children, are now indicating that the world is becoming too toxic. The resulting symptoms are indicative of this breakdown, and we are seeing more children with allergies, asthma, learning problems, behaviour problems, bedwetting, etc. My clients have found that these problems begin to disappear once the toxic load on the bodies is reduced and then eliminated.

If you have a child with ADHD, think back to when your child was younger. Did your child have processed baby foods? I know that mine did. I did not know that sugar was added to baby food. All sorts of additives are put into our foodstuffs in order to stimulate our taste buds. Please do not think that this will be so overwhelming that you will not be able to go through with the whole program. Once the body becomes stronger, you will be able to deviate periodically from the program, even during the implementation phase. If your child is accustomed to drinking soda pop on a daily basis, and will not even hear of stopping, negotiate a reduction. Even this will help to reduce the toxic load.

It is remarkable to think about the food additives and preservatives consumed by our children that we didn't consume when we were young. During the 50's, 60's and 70's "pop" was for very special occasions. When I was a vice-principal, I observed that some children in my school had soda pop every day. Do you know that carbonation affects your white blood cell activity for several hours? Do you know that one can of soda pop has ¾ cup of sugar? That it also contains caffeine? All of these ingredients have the ability to negatively affect the body.

Sometimes you may hear your children saying that "nobody loves me", "I am going to kill myself because nobody cares"; "Mommy, I hate you", etc.. It is because the body and the brain are being affected and compromised by the substances that are being consumed. The foods that go into your children's bodies can have a profound effect on their behaviour. Record in a journal, and become more knowledgeable about, your reactions and your child's reactions to various substances. Becoming aware is half the battle; the other half is eliminating the offending substance.

The information about preservatives and additives is not new. In 1978, an article in "Orthomolecular Nutrition, New Lifestyle for Super Good Health" was written regarding the effects of 'junk' food on children:

"People won't be persuaded that the deliciousness of junk pastries, pies, candies, and cold cereal is bad for them when the result of their consumption doesn't show up for a long time. Food habits are extraordinarily difficult to change. We have to resort to reason to demonstrate the relationship between junk consumption and disease at a general level first and at a personal level later. Personal demonstration is possible after you abstain from eating junk for a time. As long as you eat poorly every day, you will be ill in a low-grade way and not notice any immediate effect. After being off junk for several weeks, eating the stuff again will cause a resurgence of typical hypoglycemic symptoms. This shows the cause and effect relationship clearly and is an especially valuable lesson for children. If your child resents being put on the no-junk diet and resists your direction, it may seem sadistic, but here is a method of making your point clear: persuade your son or daughter to eat only junk for a full day a week, usually a Saturday. Let the child eat all that is desired of cold cereal coated with sugar, ice cream, chocolate bars, doughnuts with icing, etc. Feed junk food for breakfast, lunch, and dinner. Most of the time the youngster will become ill and will quickly associate sweets with sickness. Now and then there will be

a re-test required to prove the cause-and-effect relationship. If a lot of refined carbohydrate is consumed in one particular period, the lesson will be made clear."

Eating poorly every day does not produce noticeable effects quickly. That is why we often don't associate what we do with what happens in the body. One of my clients told me about the junk food diet approach and how valuable it was in order to get her teenage son to understand the connection between what he ate, and how he felt. Some of you might wish to try the 'full day junk diet' and see how your child feels. The bottom line is that it has been known for some time that 'junk' food is detrimental to one's health. <u>Eliminate all or most junk food</u>.

9) *GLUCOSE INTOLERANCE*

The body is only able to deal with a certain amount of sugar on a daily basis. If your child is ADHD (or if you are) there might well be glucose intolerance. We obtain natural sugars from vegetables, fruits, etc. Carbohydrates are turned into a sugar for fuel. Fluctuations in blood sugar can and does cause mood swings, behavioural changes and concentration problems. Sugar is in more food stuffs than you might realize. Read the section on 'sugar' later in this workbook and become more aware of the amount of sugar being consumed.

Reducing daily sugar intake makes common sense and my clients tell me that they notice a change in behaviour when this is done.

10) *ADOPTION*

Individuals, who work in foster or group homes, usually come in contact with more children who are adopted than I do. The research indicates that there is a disproportionate number of children who have been identified as ADHD from the adopted population. There are a number of reasons for this. It is speculated that young women who give their babies up for adoption, may not have taken proper care of themselves, or may have been attempting to hid their pregnancy with low food consumption.

There is much stress placed on one's body during pregnancy, and if the mother knows she is carrying a child that she will be giving up, or that she does not want, this adds to the stress. As previously stated, any stress placed on the mother's body will be felt by the developing fetus' body.

Mammals are able to determine their own mothers by smell. When a baby is born and immediately removed from the mother, it suffers a loss. Regardless of how supportive, loving, and caring the new parents may be, the child knows that it is not with its natural mother, and on a subconscious level this causes stress. It is important to point out, that this stress can definitely be overcome, but it is nonetheless another factor of which to be aware.

It is also known, that around 5 years of age, adopted children start noticing that they do not look like anybody in the family. This is a stressful situation for them, because when they finally find out they are adopted, they start questioning why their mother left them. Unfortunately, at this age, it is impossible for them to think about how difficult things might have been for the birth mother. They cannot think beyond themselves and therefore place more stress on themselves.

Around 12 years of age, adopted children start wishing for contact with their biological mother, again adding stress. We do know that not every adopted child thinks this way, however, research indicates that a large number of adopted children go through these stages, and that it leads to additional psychological and physiological stress.

11) *STRESS: EMOTIONAL, PHYSICAL, MENTAL*

Stress can come from a variety of sources. If there has been a lot of physical stress, e.g. many operations, childhood diseases, traumatic birth, etc., then the body has been 'weakened'. Entering school is often stressful. If there has already been physiological stress, then going to school may be additional stress. Often ADHD children demonstrate reactive and inappropriate behaviour, and this often causes them to be victims or to be labeled "bad".

The ways in which children perceive or judge themselves has such a dramatic effect on their abilities, both in and out of the classroom. For example, if children are consistently chosen last for teams, they start to feel that they are not good at that particular game or sport. This feeling begins to become a self-fulfilling prophecy and the more the child is chosen last, the more he believes he must be 'no good'. Children who are unable to read well stop wanting to read because it is an embarrassment. It is important to think of how the children perceive themselves and how they judge themselves, accurately or inaccurately, within this school group. They may tell you that they are the worst child in their class, even though they are not, because this is their perception.

I experienced this kind of inaccurate perception of self with my youngest daughter. When she was in grade 1, I received a phone call from the teacher two weeks after school had begun. Her teacher said that I would have to talk to Elizabeth because she did not write the math test that day. When the teacher asked her why, she simply said, "I do not wish to discuss it." Apparently Elizabeth had not completed any aspect of this math test. When she came home from school, I asked her why she didn't do her math test. She gave me a same answer, "I do not wish to discuss it." After about 15 minutes she said, "Well, if you must know mom, I didn't do it because if I didn't answer any questions, I couldn't make any mistakes and you know I'm no good at math." Where she got the idea that she was "no good" in math was beyond me. Nobody to my knowledge had told her that she was not good in math. Where would a 6 year old get the idea that she was not capable in math? She must have judged herself according to the math abilities of others.

How many of our children make decisions about themselves that are erroneous? And we, as parents, don't even have an opportunity to correct them. How many times have they watched TV and judged themselves to be 'less good' than the kids on TV? We have to start thinking about our children and their developmental stages and what they really can handle. Most of them can't handle very much and really do need to be protected and nurtured for a lot longer than we may currently think. As parents you can help by talking with them and asking about their perception of an experience, and correcting any inaccurate perceptions that might have resulted.

As mentioned earlier, stress comes in three forms: physical, mental, and emotional. How much and what types of stress has your child's (or your) body had to cope with? Stress, from whatever source, can, and does, put an extra burden on the body. In order to deal with the negative burden, sufficient nutrients need to be available. If they are not, the body begins to show signs of weakness. We all know that life is not stress free, but we must give our bodies the ability to handle the stress. A good daily activity is to introduce a quiet time. The whole family can have quiet time, even for just 20 minutes. This will help to reduce the stress. When you start the supplemental component of this program, you will begin to build strength within the body. Removing junk food from the daily routine will also reduce stress. By reducing stress you can change the way in which your (or your child's) body and brain function, and ultimately, change the way in which you (or your child) behave and learn.

12) *DIET*

Diet was briefly reviewed in the preservative/additives factor, but will be elaborated upon here. Take some time to think about what your child (or you), eat during the day. Do you think your child has had an optimal diet? Do you think you have had an optimal diet? If you, or your child, have been eating mostly processed food (foods that have been altered during the processing stage), then it is apparent that the diet is not optimal. Even if you, or your child, has had an optimal diet, there may be a number of other factors from this list that cause the optimal diet to be insufficient to override all of the other factors. The diet of today is not like it was 50 years ago. Our food supply has been reduced in nutrient value. Even though you may be preparing your own meals, the foods you cook with have a lower nutritional value than they did many years ago. This is yet another reason for supplementing our bodies. It has also been found that we need to be taking digestive enzymes. Digestive enzymes help our bodies digest food properly.

Many of my clients have indicated that they do not (or their child does not) eat breakfast, or that 'sugared' cereals are preferred over other foods. If the body is not being supplied with proper 'fuel', it cannot work properly. Start keeping a written list of all the food your child is consuming. Statistics state that Americans annually consume 130 pounds of sugar. Too much sugar is hard on our bodies and it's added to most canned, packaged, and processed foods. If child's (or your) diet has been less that desirable, then you must consider that this has had an impact on your child's (or your own) system.

My clients tell me that within the first month of implementing the program their child's eating habits improved. Moderating one's diet is a common sense approach. Don't worry if your child does not start to eat differently immediately. The supplements will help change this pattern.

13) *LACK OF EXERCISE*

Many ADHD children or adults do not have the desire to exercise. Unfortunately, a lack of exercise does not allow the lymphatic system to rid the body of toxins. Physical activity does not mean being in perpetual motion, but rather, being involved in an activity that will strengthen the body. I am told by qualified fitness instructors, that walking, hiking, and biking are excellent activities. See how simple and enjoyable it can be. Many of my clients noted that it took about 3 to 4 months before their child showed an interest in physical activity.

Most of us do not think about our lymphatic systems and yet this system is one of the most important. It is responsible for transporting toxic wastes out of our bodies. Walking and hiking stimulate the lymphatic pumps behind the knees and hence, help the lymphatic system do its job.

It is speculated that we are seeing more overweight children because their diet is deficient in necessary nutrients, they over-consume junk food, and they don't get enough exercise. The body cannot use all of the fuel from food at once, so it stores it in the fat cells for future use. Also, toxins in the blood can cause a multitude of problems, including behaviour and learning problems. It is therefore important for you to give the body a chance to clean and heal itself. Feed it well, take supplements, exercise, and drink plenty of water.

14) *INSUFFICIENT NUTRIENTS*

If our diet is poor, it becomes difficult to obtain sufficient nutrients. But it goes beyond that. Not only do we receive insufficient nutrients; our digestion becomes compromised due to the amount of processed foods being consumed. If you eat processed foods, the digestive enzymes in your body have a difficult time 'breaking down' the foods. When this happens, much of the food goes undigested from the stomach to the intestines where it putrefies or ferments. When this occurs your intestines may become full of undigested food. Bacteria in the intestines will continue to break it down for elimination but if the use of antibiotics has been frequent, the likelihood exists that the number of 'friendly' bacteria may not be sufficient to properly do the job. If this is the case, the 'bad' bacteria may have a chance to step in. The body attempts to keep the 'bad' bacteria in check, however, we must help.

Bad body odour that does not respond to bathing is likely coming from the waste build up in the intestines. The 'sewer' smell is emitted from the pores. Imagine how difficult it must be for a child who 'smells' or who has excessive gas. No one wants to be near him/her, thus causing socializing problems, which ultimately affect self-esteem.

One thing parents can do to help their children, is to teach them to chew their food more thoroughly, because digestion actually begins in the mouth. Chewing food more thoroughly makes it easier for the stomach to do its job of digesting it. Digestive enzymes are necessary for the digestion of our food. Eating processed food causes more digestive enzymes to be used in the process of digesting. The human body only has a certain number of these enzymes. Taking plant/digestive enzymes before eating will greatly assist the body's digestive ability.

15) CHEMICAL SENSITIVITIES

Review the section on "chemical sensitivities" later in this workbook to help you make more associations.

Think about all the toys, furnishings, equipment, etc., that may be in your child's room. Reduce the exposure. Watch your child's (or your own) reaction to new clothes, new toys, to a newly-painted room, to gasoline, to perfume, etc. Eliminate as many chemicals as possible from your home. Today's marketplace is making changes with many products being non-toxic. If you or your child has difficulty reading new books, it may be that the printing chemicals are causing the problem.

One 17 year old client was initially so uncooperative and non-compliant that I wondered if I might be of any help. It took three sessions in the presence of his parent, to finally gain his attention and trust. I now know that it would have been easier, and perhaps better, to first start him on the supplemental component of the program, and then complete the educational and elimination components.

Over the course of the three sessions, however, we covered all of this material and discovered that he was having difficulty with certain chemicals; that his diet was terrible; that he was failing all subjects; that he was living with friends because he couldn't/wouldn't follow house rules; and, that he had constant and unexplained aches and pains. When he finally realized that his body and brain were not functioning properly, due to poor diet and chemical sensitivities, he agreed to try the program and to move home. Within four months, he had improved his grades to B's and C's and was looking forward to a drug-free existence - which occurred in the fifth month.

From age 14 to 17, he had created his own masterpiece by turning his bedroom walls into a collage of pictures taken from magazines. While it may have been visually appealing, it was a chemical nightmare: ink fixatives, etc. are used in the production of magazine pictures. He was constantly being exposed to many chemicals. His parents and I convinced him to sleep in another room while his bedroom was 'aired' out.

16) *EXCESSIVE SENSORY STIMULATION*

All of the students in my research group had difficulty with excessive noise, excessive activity, and were not able to concentrate within such an environment. It has been found that deficiencies in B vitamins are associated with symptoms such as noise sensitivity.

Excessive sensory stimulation may start as early as infancy. While stimulation is necessary, too much may become problematic. Knowing the boundaries seems to be the challenge.

Today's child often watches too much TV, uses the computer too much, and may be surrounded by constant noise. The human body can only endure so much stimulation and noise before it starts to show signs of weakness. Adults can make wise choices, opting for a quiet evening, a quiet hobby, etc.. Children need to be taught how to be quiet and how to enjoy quiet activities. Model this skill for your child. Start by having a daily period of quiet time.

Some of my clients indicated that their children were noise sensitive. A breaking balloon, the backfire of a car, even a loud noise, would cause the child to start crying or trembling. After one month on the program, clients reported that these symptoms were significantly reduced; or in some cases, disappeared. Ask yourself the following question: How much, and how frequently, does my child watch TV? You may not have thought about how the brain or the central nervous system responds to the constant changing of images, light, colour, sound etc. Bombardment may be an appropriate word. Consider moderating daily activities and cut down on exposure.

Dr. Jane Healey (author of Endangered Minds) states that she is concerned about the development of our children's minds due to the influx and use of computers by young children. A good balance between toys that require creativity, problem solving, and social interaction should be part of the child's routine. Computers are great tools, but should not replace other forms of learning.

Always remember that there are situations over which we have no control, e.g. outside environmental noises and workplace noises, but we do have control over our own 'space'. Make it a peaceful haven if you can. The benefits outweigh the effort.

QUESTIONNAIRES

1. **Revealing Health Factors for Growth and Behaviour**
2. **Determining the Possible Effect of Allergies and/or Vitamin/ Mineral Deficiencies**

If you are an adult completing the questionnaires, please provide answers where you can. You may find it useful to involve your spouse, your parents, or other relatives in the answering of the questions. All of the answers give insight into what has been causing you or your child to be unable to make academic progress in keeping with his/her ability, and unable to behave properly.

Clients have told me that by working through the questionnaires, many memories were triggered which enabled them to complete the analysis. If you are finding that your memories are not being prompted by the following questions, continue to read the material until some connections are made, or until some information acts "like a lightning rod".

Revealing Health Factors for Growth and Behaviour

Indicate your child's (your) birth weight [_____]. Was your baby pre-term? ☐ Low birth weight? ☐ Adopted? ☐Was there anything unusual about the pregnancy [prolonged or frequent sickness, an accident, abnormal stress or trauma, drug taking (medication by prescription, over-the-counter medications, recreational drugs) etc.]?

List and describe any recurring medical problems (which required medication and/or an operation) that you/your child had prior to 5 years of age (i.e. ear aches, colds, sore throats, stomach aches, accidents, etc.)

State what was done to eliminate the problem(s):

Does your child suffer from bedwetting? NO / YES (circle one)
If YES, for how long? _
What was done to correct the problem?

Did your child's health and behaviour improve between the ages of 0-5? ☐ or 5+? ☐

Do you/your child suffer from allergies? NO /YES (circle one) If YES, to what?

Are you, or is your child, on medication for allergies at the present time? NO / YES (circle one) If YES, list the type(s) of medication.

If you were (or your child was) previously on medication for an allergy, please indicate WHEN, for HOW LONG, and the TYPE OF MEDICATION used.

What approaches have you taken to provide relief for yourself/your child?

How has your/your child's behaviour, or lack of school progress affected your home environment, interpersonal relations, and your approach to parenting?

This process may be frustrating at times, but remember that you are trying to reveal past events which have contributed to the present labeling of ADHD. Be patient. Work through the process and you will begin to see the links that exist between health and learning, and between health and behaviour. *Often the earliest symptoms of the problem start to show in the early years. If this is the case, it will take a longer time to see more permanent results.*

My clients have told me that physical and behavioral improvements most noticed within the first three months after implementing the program, are the following:

- Appears to be calmer
- Is more co-operative
- Wakes more refreshed
- Appears to be less tired during the day
- Does not complain of aches and pains as frequently
- Has lost (if originally overweight) or gained weight
- Overall health seems to be improving
- Dark circles under the eyes seem to have diminished

The purpose of the following Questionnaire is to provide you with a list of the most commonly observed ADHD symptoms, and provide you an opportunity to record your observations. Physical symptoms present themselves first, often in infancy or prior to 5 years of age. During the detoxification or healing stage, these physical symptoms are usually the first to respond, diminish in frequency and then disappear.

It is not mandatory for you to include the age at which you first noticed these symptoms, but if you can recall the age, this will certainly help you establish a more accurate timeline for the development of the disorder. For instance, if your child experienced sleeping problems which began in infancy, then it is reasonable to expect that 'something' was agitating his/her body (system), preventing him/her from gaining the restful sleep so necessary. Some of my clients state that their babies never slept for more than a couple of hours at a time. Experts in the field of allergies suggest that food substances and/or environmental substances can have an effect on the body, so that the body cannot possibly be relaxed enough for rest to occur.

Determining the Possible Effect of Allergies and/or Vitamin/ Mineral Deficiencies

This exercise of identifying your (or your child's) characteristics, provides you with a record. Once you begin the program, review these lists of characteristics on a monthly basis and note where improvement has occurred. Later on in the workbook, you will learn about the symptoms of vitamin and mineral deficiencies. Many characteristics associated with ADHD are the same as the symptoms for vitamin and mineral deficiencies.

These characteristics or symptoms were compiled from the academic and medical records of the students in my research group. Not all children experienced the same symptoms, but all children shared many similar ones.

PHYSICAL SYMPTOMS	Age	Yes	No
Disturbed sleeping pattern			
Dislikes to be touched or cuddled			
Constantly tired and fatigued			
Glazed or glassy look to eyes			
Has/had convulsions			
Hives and/or strong reaction to bee sings or insects bites			
Gibberish speech			
Complains of constant aches and pains, recurring headaches and/or stomach aches			
Frequent ear aches, colds, sore throats			
Pale complexion, yet pronounced red cheeks			
Rashes on arms, legs or other parts of the body that do not clear up			
Constantly yawning or rubbing of eyes or ears			
Drooling after infancy			
Speech problems noted (i.e. lisping, stuttering)			
Poor sense of balance			
Unusual gait (i.e. shuffling, walking on toes)			
Difficulty copying words from a book or the blackboard			
Craving for, or intense dislike of, certain foods or drinks			
Poor manual dexterity			
Underweight/overweight			
Hearing loss			
Constant sniffling, blinking and squinting			

PHYSICAL SYMPTOMS	Age	Yes	No
Complains of ringing in the ears			
Red eyes or dark circles, or 'bags' under the eyes			
Blurred vision			
Constant coughing			
Abdominal cramps and diarrhea experienced			
Sleeping, or drowsy spells, after meals			
Cravings for candy, soda pop or coffee, between meals, or mid-afternoon			
Bad dreams, nightmares, night terrors			
Hungry between meals, or at night			
Fatigue relieved by eating			
Rough patches on face, arms, stomach, legs			
Mentally, emotionally cruel towards parent(s)			
Excessive sweating			
Trembling of the hands			
Bleeding gums			
Allergies: asthma, hay fever, skin rash, sinus trouble			
Faint if meal is delayed			
Irritable before meals			
Slow starter in the morning			
High strung			
Bruises easily			
Itchy, dry skin			
Change in handwriting noted during day, or when completing assignments			

PHYSICAL SYMPTOMS	Age	Yes	No
Pimples, acne			
Twitching of muscles			
Crossed eyes, doesn't see well, or has one weak eye			
Picks nose, thick discharge, postnasal drip			
Constant clearing of throat			
Bad breath, mouth breather, swollen glands			
Canker sore, bad teeth, or grinding of teeth			
Chest hurts, heart races for no apparent reason, feels faint, wheezes when breathing			
Smelly feet			
Excessive gas			
Strong body odour that doesn't respond to bathing			
Frequent vomiting, nausea			
Car sickness			
Red eyes when reading			
Sleepy all the time			
Projectile vomiting			
Rough hands			
Cracked skin on feet or between toes			

In my research and subsequent work, I found that most of the children and adults labeled ADHD have had more than two (sometimes as many as four or five) antibiotic prescriptions per year.

While thought to be necessary by your physician, it is now known that the antibiotics change the balance between good and bad bacteria in the intestines which can contribute to digestive problems and nutritional deficiencies.

BEHAVIOURAL SYMPTOMS	Age	Yes	No
Impulsiveness			
Very stubborn or strong willed			
Inconsistent mood swings			
'Spaced out' appearance			
Aggressive behavior			
Poor social skills			
Restlessness			
Demonstrates a more *negative* than *positive* attitude			
Carelessness about self and things			
Laziness			
Making animal noises for no reason			
On Ritalin™ or other psycho stimulant			
Temper tantrums after the age of 5			
Reluctance to complete tasks			
Frequently interrupts or speaks out without regard for others			
Uncooperative attitude			
Hostile attitude			
Lack of leadership observed			
Feelings of inadequacy, insecurity and loneliness			
Difficulty in making and keeping friends			
Demonstrated 'follower' tendencies			
Frequent depression noted			
Little regard for neatness in person or work			
Tendency to regress under pressure			
Tendency to be manipulative			
Disrespect for others			

BEHAVIOURAL SYMPTOMS	Age	Yes	No
Little concern for consequences or disciplinary threats			
Distant and unable to relate emotionally to those around			
Moodiness, cries easily			
Magnification on insignificant details			
Phobias (excessive fear of some thing or situation)			
Jealousy			
Favours one parent over the other			
Nervous habits, compulsive behaviours			
Turns night into day			
Washing of hands, cracking knuckles, playing with matches, eating clothes, constantly putting things into mouth, nail biting, picking at clothes, separating food on plate, stealing			
Physically violent towards parent(s), siblings			

COGNITIVE SYMPTOMS	Age	Yes	No
Distractible			
Short attention span			
Lack of concentration			
Appearance of impaired hearing			
Inconsistent learning - knows something today and then does not know it tomorrow			
Auditory or visual memory weakness			

COGNITIVE SYMPTOMS	Age	Yes	No
Difficulty with written expression, poor letter formation, difficulty writing thoughts logically on paper			
Difficulty remembering requests			
Slower or faster progress for walking or talking, (e.g. ran at 9 months of age, walked around 16-20 months, talked around 3 years of age)			
Diagnosed as "Learning Disabled"			
Difficulty with reading			
Frequent letter reversal			
Fearful, overwhelmed by people, places, or things			
Decisions not made easily			
Difficulty remembering words even after much review			

Once you uncover the factors that may have contributed to the development of ADHD symptoms for you (or your child), please turn to the Supplementation Section and learn which supplements you should purchase. Begin the supplementation component of the program and, if this is all you are capable of doing right now, simply stay with the supplements and continue reviewing the information in the workbook.

When you are ready, review the Elimination component of the program and begin eliminating junk food, sugar products, and milk from your child's (or your) diet.

On the following pages you will find a series of symptoms that have been linked to allergies and deficiencies. It has often been speculated that vitamin and mineral deficiencies initiate some of the symptoms associated with various disorders. Cognitive impairment and poor behaviour are two of the areas dramatically improved through the use of supplements. Allergies have also been implicated in learning and behaviour disorders, and there are countless research papers to attest to this.

Allergies

Common Signs of a Hidden Allergy

All parents should become aware and informed about the many factors affecting children's ability to learn and to behave in a socially acceptable way. Food allergy and/or chemical exposure are two of the many factors that affect children's ability to learn and to behave.

Parents are encouraged to seek information and gain an understanding from a wide variety of books that are available.

Sometimes it is difficult to determine if there were indicators of allergies in your child or yourself. Many clients have shared with me that their children had been tested for a number of allergies, and none were found. Oftentimes a substance may pose a problem, but has not yet reached the "allergic" stage. Food intolerances are usually observed prior to allergy. While you are reading through the various allergy symptoms associated with different age groups, you may wish to check off those relevant to you or your child. If you are an adult with ADHD, ask your parents about your childhood and go through the list with them. If this is not possible, or you do not wish to have them involved, simply use your own memory and make notes accordingly. If you cannot remember back to your childhood, do not worry, and simply focus on the adolescent and adult symptoms; often if you are having some problems relating to foods and substances now, you probably exhibited certain symptoms as a child.

Being aware of the possible factors causing a learning or behaviour problem will help the parent to seek the most advantageous treatment program. If you are the adult seeking knowledge, consider the following in reference to yourself.

These signs indicate the possibility of a hidden allergy:

- Above-average ability/ below-average results and progress
- Aggressive, hostile, anti-social behaviours
- Hearing problems
- Non-compliance with requests
- Rough skin, dark eye circles, red ears, running nose
- A high-pitched voice
- Sleep disorders such as night terrors, nightmares, insomnia
- Occurrence of bedwetting after 5 years of age
- Speaking gibberish
- Colic
- Rashes
- Loose bowels
- Frequent colds
- Irritability
- Chronic cough
- Diaper rash, redness at anus or on cheeks
- Cold sore
- Fussy eater
- Hives or welts
- Nose rubbing
- Tiny broken blood vessels under the skin
- Bronchitis
- Eczema
- Wheezing
- Bloodshot eyes
- Nasal stuffiness, sniffling, snorting, sneezing

Also, many of the same factors that result in ear infections, bedwetting and colic contribute to hyperactivity, short attention span, behavioural and learning problems.

Some of the factors indicating hyperactivity are:
- Poor nutrition and faulty digestion

- Food allergies and intolerance
- Environmental toxins
- Yeast overgrowth and parasites
- Repeated antibiotics and other medications

CHILDHOOD ALLERGIES

ALLERGIES BEFORE BIRTH - SYMPTOMS:

- Very active - a 'kicker'

ALLERGIES DURING INFANCY - SYMPTOMS:

- Colicky
- Pushed bottle away but would eat food
- Irritability, poor sleep patterns, prolonged crying
- Fainting spells, excessive drool, perspiration
- Liked to be walked or bounced constantly
- Ear infections
- Nasal congestion and bronchiolitis (early form of asthma), wheezing sounds, noisy chest
- Nose mucus

ALLERGIES IN TODDLERS - SYMPTOMS:

- Reacts explosively to the word "No"
- Dark eye circles, read ear lobes, wiggly legs, unfocused look to eyes.

ALLERGIES IN OLDER CHILDREN - SYMPTOMS:

- May cough when starting to run, laugh or exercise
- May begin to develop behavioural and learning problems such as hitting, kicking, spitting, restlessness, inability to concentrate

- May exhibit schizophrenic personality
- May become withdrawn, crawl under furniture, not like to be touched
- May make suicidal statements which indicate allergic fatigue, e.g. wishing to be dead, "nobody loves me" statements
- May experience bladder spasm, wet bed or underwear, or race for the toilet
- Bloating, belching and passing of gas rectally - occurs when stomach separates the foods that cause trouble from those that do not
- Belly aches, headaches, leg aches
- Colitis
- Eczema, rashes in the creases of the arms and legs

Children with untreated food allergies may suffer frequent ear aches, eczema, bedwetting, asthma, hyperactivity, learning or discipline problems, etc. Adults whose allergies are left untreated may have frequent headaches, 'spaciness', spells of sleepiness, arthritic symptoms, hypoglycemic symptoms, frequent infections, etc.

Both children and adults may experience outbursts of temper as a result of untreated food allergy. Some clients have experienced problems with the following items:
- Red licorice
- Milk and milk products
- Preservatives
- Gum

ALLERGIES IN ADOLESCENTS- SYMPTOMS:

- Headaches, fatigue, irritability, depression (allergic teenagers may become depressed rather than develop hay fever or asthma)
- Bloating, gas, diarrhea, constipation or belching (likely indicates lactose intolerance or milk allergy)
- Recurring ear aches, leg aches, congestion, noises related to mucus or irritation in the throat causing a throaty sound or even a clucking noise, indicate the possibility of a milk allergy

ALLERGIES IN ADULTS - SYMPTOMS:

- Blood in stool (e.g. irritable bowel, Crone's disease or Ulcerative Colitis), as determined by a physician
- Many experts believe that these aforementioned problems are the result of: bladder problems, high blood pressure, irregular heartbeat, arteriosclerosis, arthritis, manic depression

WITHDRAWAL REACTIONS FROM ALLERGIES

Withdrawal reactions occur after stimulatory ones. Stimulation resulting in excitability can be considered an adaptive response by the body to some environmental substance. When the body can no longer adapt, it enters the various stages of imbalance. These are withdrawal reactions, also called hangovers or letdowns. Short-term adverse symptoms are experienced when a person avoids a substance to which he/she is allergic or addicted. There are varying degrees of withdrawal reactions and they are described for you below.

Minus 1 reactions are mainly physical symptoms, commonly called allergic reactions. They include: running nose, coughing, wheezing, asthma, itching, hives, eczema, excessive gas, diarrhea, constipation, colitis and other localized physical problems.

Minus 2 reactions are systemic allergic symptoms, affecting not just one, but many, parts of the body. A person in this stage of allergy is typically tired, dopey, sleepy or mildly depressed. He/she is frequently plagued by painful syndromes such as, headaches, neck aches, back aches and neuralgia. This is the phase in which chest pains and cardiovascular effects are noticed. Cardiovascular symptoms can include: rapid or irregular pulse or heartbeat, hypertension, phlebitis, anemia or tendencies toward bleeding and bruising. In Minus 2 reaction state, physical fatigue, head ache, and muscle/joint aches and pains, including arthritis are commonly seen. Fatigue, when related to food allergy, tends to be worse in the morning. Allergic fatigue is seemingly without case, and is not ordinarily relieved by periods of rest.

Minus 3 reactions are characterized by mental exhaustion. In the extreme case, symptoms include: confused thinking, indecisiveness, moodiness, sadness, being withdrawn, apathy and low concentration. Attention, emotional stability, comprehension and thought processes are also impaired. Aphasia (the inability to speak or to find words for things), mental lapses, and blackouts, may also occur in this reaction stage.

Minus 4 reactions are characterized by severe depression. While depression does occur in the young, it is most commonly found in the middle-aged or elderly person who has had a lifetime to develop to this stage. Many other factors have been thought to be the causative agent of depressions, but it is often caused by a lifelong addiction to common foods, drinks, and environmental chemicals.

There is nothing static about any of these reaction stages. A person may move from one stage to another and from stimulatory to withdrawal phases as the problem develops.

Foods that cause violent symptoms must be eliminated from the diet completely for a minimum of 30 days. Avoiding a food allergen allows one's body to revert back to a more normal state, which may initially be uncomfortable. These feelings of discomfort are withdrawal symptoms. You may also have a strong craving for the food that you are eliminating, however, this will likely only last a few days, and then you or your child will feel better.

All foods can cause reactions, but some are more potent than others. Protein foods are more allergenic than "non-protein" foods because proteins are more difficult to digest than fats or carbohydrates.

Reintroducing the food on a frequent basis will likely produce similar problems as before. Moderation should be followed. Some people never eliminate an allergic response to certain foods. This has become known as fixed food sensitivity, and you should consider not allowing these foods in your diet.

It took me 6 months to eliminate a corn allergy, during which time I experienced the strong craving for popcorn. I did the elimination trial in 3-month increments and found it helpful to keep a journal, to track my symptoms, as I reintroduced corn into my diet.

CHEMICAL SENSITIVITIES

Over 500 billion chemicals are manufactured in North America each year, 500,000 of which are in common use. These chemicals have found their way into our homes, our food, our water, our air, and ultimately our bodies. Chemicals and their cumulative effects have a serious impact on our health.

Chemicals enter our body through the mouth and nose, and through direct contact. Chemically sensitive people acquire their susceptibility because of hereditary and genetic factors, lowered immunity, and inadequate or damaged body detoxification mechanisms. Chemical susceptibility usually develops as a result of repeated, low-level exposure to a chemical over a period of time; however, a chemical sensitivity may be triggered by a massive, overwhelming exposure to a chemical spill, fire, pesticide sprays, or general anesthesia.

TYPES OF CHEMICAL EXPOSURES

- Indoor chemical air contaminants
- Outdoor chemical air contaminants
- Chemical contaminants of food and water
- Drugs and medications
- Clothing and personal care products

TYPES OF CHEMICAL REACTIONS

Experts state that reactions to chemical allergens may be seen as part of a maladaptive process. When susceptible people are exposed to chemicals, their bodies adapt after the first exposure and no symptoms are obvious.

Repeated exposure to chemicals may produce chronic symptoms. The resulting cumulative damage generally leads to a gradual decline in health. Rashes, hives, and skin eruptions are symptoms common to this type of reaction. Some chemical reactions go undetected because they don't produce obvious, overt symptoms.

The toxicity of most chemicals is determined by animal studies. While these studies are helpful, they are not absolute. Animal physiology differs from human physiology; therefore the effects of a chemical may be very different in the human population. Human drug doses that are simply extrapolated from animal studies, based on the weight of the animal, may not be accurate. Perhaps the chemically sensitive people in our society can be likened to the canaries of the coal mine during the last century. Death of the birds would indicate that there was a deadly presence of methane gas. The miners heeded this warning and the mine was closed. We can then say that chemically sensitive people are the sensors of our polluted air, water, and food. They produce the early warning signs indicating that we must clean up our home and work environments. The chemically sensitive are those who have experienced overexposure, or subtle, cumulative exposure to harmful chemicals, which have damaged their detoxification pathways and immune system. There are many nutritional supplements that help to detoxify the body's symptoms.

Symptoms of Chemical Sensitivities

The first organ, and the most easily affected by chemicals, is the brain. Chemicals are deposited in fat cells, and the brain has a very high fat content. Smooth muscle is also easily affected by food and chemical sensitivities; however, any system can be affected. Repeated exposure to offending foods or chemicals can result in chronic symptoms and illness.

Cerebral Symptoms:
*confusion *depression *anger *brain exhaustion *inability to concentrate *apathy *emotional *instability *mental fatigue *light-headed *lethargy

Respiratory Symptoms:
*coughing *bronchitis *asthma *"air hunger"

Gastrointestinal and Urinary Symptoms:
*excessive thirst *eating or drinking binges *diarrhea *constipation *urgency and frequency of urination *nausea *vomiting *gas *dry mouth, *bad or metallic taste in the mouth *abdominal pain *difficulty swallowing *heartburn *gallbladder symptoms

Neurological Symptoms:
*headaches *neck aches *nerve pain *muscle pain *arthritis *chest pain *fainting *restless legs *numbness

Ear, Nose and Throat Symptoms:
*ringing in the ears *dizziness *cough *itching inside the ears *hypersensitivity to noise *rhinitis *nasal obstruction *stuffy nose

Skin Symptoms:
*hives *acne *blisters *eczema *itching *burning

Eye Symptoms:
*vision disturbances *watery eyes *light sensitivity *eye pain *swelling around eyes and drooping eyelids *itching *swollen red eyelids

Musculoskeletal Symptoms:
*fatigue *muscle pain *cramps *weakness *joint pain *stiffness *lack of co-ordination

Chemically susceptible people can become accustomed to chemicals, thereby not reacting upon exposure. This is called "masking". For example, sensitive persons can always identify fresh paint as a problem because it is not often encountered, but they may not recognize that the odour from a gas range is problematic because they are exposed to it daily and have become "masked".

If they avoid all natural gas exposures for 4 - 7 days, symptoms will appear upon their return to the natural gas sources.

Chemically susceptible people may be addicted to chemicals, just as food-sensitive people are addicted to allergenic foods. Those who are chemically addicted may say they love the smell of gasoline, nail polish, or fabric softener.

Chemically sensitive people have an extremely acute sense of smell, and are more aware of odours and chemicals than those unaffected, however, they may not detect the chemical or odour that is triggering a reaction. When exposed to chemicals, sensitive persons should always breathe through their mouths, since chemical fumes entering the nose can directly affect the brain through interconnecting nerve pathways. Chemicals entering the body through the mouth must circulate through the bloodstream and pass through the blood-brain barrier before affecting the brain. Some exposure to chemicals occurs without us being aware. Many symptoms may be the result of exposure to a chemical or chemicals. Reflect on how you or your child reacts to perfumes, cleaning products, hair sprays, air fresheners, etc.

DEALING WITH CHEMICAL SENSITIVITIES

- Clean up the interior environment of your home and place of work. Remove all chemically-based cleaning products from your home. Store them in the garage if necessary. Since there are so many natural cleaning products available today, it is unnecessary to pollute your home.
- Eat a diet of clean food, uncontaminated by pesticides, fertilizers or processing. Purchase foods that are free from pesticides and fertilizers. Always wash produce before eating it. A good washing solution consists of food-safe hydrogen peroxide and water.
- Drink only safe, uncontaminated water. Drink distilled water if possible. If not, at least filter your tap water by using a system such as Brita ™.
- Use an air cleaner both at home and in your car, not an air freshener.
- Provide nutritional support for your immune system. Certain vitamins and minerals (i.e. vitamin E and selenium) will help remove chemicals from the body. Some companies sell supplements specifically formulated to remove chemical deposits in the blood.

Implementing these measures requires some thought and effort, but by doing so you will be reducing the toxic load on your immune system.

Easy Ways to Begin Detoxifying

- Wash clothes in borax and use vinegar as the softener, or use a product that is free of chemicals.
- Remove as many chemical cleaners from your home as possible, use vinegar and water to clean as long as no one has an allergy to vinegar.
- Remove scented products from your home and avoid heavily perfumed areas.
- Remove carpets and other synthetic materials from the bedroom of the sensitive person or child.
- Mouthwash, tooth paste, and even some soaps can cause problems, so it is wise to use the most basic products; these are even cheaper (e.g. baking soda for teeth). Avoid products that contain glycerin as it can be damaging to delicate skin tissues.
- Cook as many meals as possible from basic ingredients, in order to avoid preservatives and additives.
- When saving leftovers, store food in glass containers, as chemicals can be leached into food from plastic ones. The most recent research indicates that leftovers have little or no nutritional value after withstanding two periods of cooking. If, out of economic necessity, you cannot afford to dispose of extra food, at least serve it with a freshly prepared portion.

OTHER ENVIRONMENTAL PROBLEMS

These questions are intended to heighten your awareness with regards to the different substances in your environment and how they may have affected you or your child. If you answer 'yes' or can relate to many of the questions, then this may have been a factor impacting the immune system.

Consider the following:
- Is your home old or new? (Old homes may have more molds, dust, mildew, etc, while new homes will likely be 'outgassing' chemicals from new appliances, carpet, cupboards, paint, flooring, etc.)
- How long have you been living there? How old was your child when you moved into your home?
- Were renovations done during pregnancy or just after birth of a child? How many renovations have been done during the time of living in the home?
- How often and when have you purchased new furniture?
- What is the proximity of your house to major highways and/or factories?
- How did/does your child behave in an enclosed mall?
- How does your child react to perfume, gasoline, softeners, paint, varnishes, etc.?
- Does your child react to new clothes or the tags in new cloths (i.e. itching)?
- Does your child's behaviour change when in, or around chlorinated pools?
- Have you or your child shown a reaction of any kind to cleaning products used in the home or at school?

- Do you live in a highly polluted area?
- What potential chemical or toxic problems exist in your (or your child's) bedroom?
- Where were you and your spouse working when your child was conceived? What kind of exposure might you have encountered during pregnancy?
- Did anything occur in your immediate area just before or just after your child was born? (i.e. chemical spills, etc.)
- Did your child get 'gassed' in early years? (i.e. exposed to herbicides, pesticides, etc.)
- Is smoking permitted in the home? How frequently, and by whom?

Remember:
New building materials have a high chemical content
New furniture has been treated with chemicals
Old houses may have lead-based paint
Old houses may be moldy or musty in certain areas

Foods, dust, mildews, pollen and chemicals usually start to cause problems by 2, 3, 4, years of age. If chemical sensitivity is a problem, you will note that your child smells chemicals before anyone else, or gets sick when riding in cars.

PRESERVATIVES

Preservatives can have a detrimental effect on the body, often because the body does not know how to digest and utilize them. The following information will provide a general understanding about preservatives.

About 100 chemicals called "anti-spoilants" are used to help prevent microbiological growth and chemical deterioration in our food. They include: antioxidants, "mold" inhibitors, fungicides and sequestering agents. Other general purpose preservatives are: sulphur dioxide and pro-pylgallate. Preservatives prevent changes affecting colour, flavour, texture, or appearance. Traditional preservatives include salt, sugar, vinegar, spices, and wood smoke, however, **wood smoke is no longer considered safe**. Adding chemicals to food began when it was first discovered that 'salting' meat would make it last longer.

Over 10,000 intentional additives are currently used in foods. Many people are allergic to even the smallest amounts of these compounds. Inconsistent labeling makes it difficult to determine whether the offending substances have been added to food. If in doubt, always write to the packer or manufacturer and explain that you have allergies and must know more about the product in order to be able to use it. If you cannot pronounce the listed ingredients, don't buy it.

The laws governing packaging and food processing state that labels must:

- Identify the product in a language the consumer can understand.
- Identify the manufacturer, packer, or distributor.

- Declare the quantity of contents, either in net weight or volume.
- List the ingredients in order of predominance. An item that lists sugar first or second will have very high sugar content.
- Accurately represent the contents of the container, if a picture of the product is used on the label.

In some cases, relatively few food additives need to be listed on labels. For over 300 "standard" foods (those for which the government has written chemical recipes) no ingredients need be listed. Manufacturers can choose among many alternative standard chemicals without having to indicate on the label which is used. Only if the processor substitutes or adds a non-standard chemical must they indicate that fact on the label. Similarly, if monosodium glutamate (MSG) is used in canned vegetables, it must appear on the label, but it may be added to mayonnaise and salad dressings without being listed if a standard recipe is followed. It is impossible for consumers to know whether the absence of additives on a label means that none are present, or whether it means the food is covered by a standard recipe and contains numerous additives. For this reason, purchasing the freshest foods possible is always the safest route to take.

Consumer demand for uniform appearance and flavour in food products has played a large role in increased use of food additives in recent years. To meet this demand, food processors and manufacturers are increasingly using more additives. Most are unfamiliar chemicals with no nutritional value. Some additives are quite harmless, but the safety of others is in question. Frequently, additives are used to conceal the inferior quality of food, to heighten the appearance of damaged food, or to make the food more attractive to the consumer.

Chemical additives used in food processing must make the food more easily available for distribution purposes, improve its shelf life, increase quality or customer acceptability, or facilitate the foods manufacture or preparation.

READING LABELS

Since we live in a society where both parents usually work, it would be nearly impossible to assume that everyone would have the time to make all of their meals from scratch. Because of this, we need to become more aware as consumers, and make the best choices that we can. When we increase our awareness, the number of choices we have seems to increase dramatically. Reading food labels will enable you to decide whether or not particular brands will be appropriate for your family. This may seem like a time consuming task (and in the beginning it may take a little bit longer), but it will soon become very easy for you to determine which products you wish to purchase.

The first task in reading labels is to identify any food which is an allergen. Foods may be listed by their common names, or they may be described by their "food component" names. For example, zein, which is corn protein, appears on labels, as does whey, which is a milk component.

Reading labels can also help to determine the presence of food additives that may cause reactions. A food additive is a substance or mixture that has been added to aid in production, processing, packaging, or storing of the food.

The safest foods for allergic people to eat are fresh, organically grown fruits, vegetables, and meats, however, we are forced to buy commercially processed foods, because many of us are unable to grow our own food, and top-quality food is not always available. It is important to learn to read food labels intelligently, to recognize food additives, and to use this information to make wise food purchases. Many people have adopted the rule that if they cannot pronounce the names of ingredients, they don't buy the product.

Artificial Sweeteners

Artificial sweeteners are non-nutritive, non-caloric sweeteners that have been synthesized in a laboratory. They are intended to help decrease sugar and calorie intake, and to be safe for diabetics. However artificial sweeteners increase appetite in general and interfere with the taste, enjoyment, and satisfaction obtained from eating foods high in complex carbohydrates. They also increase preference for fat intake and interfere with our body's ability to select foods containing the nutrients it needs. The following are examples of artificial sweeteners that you might choose to avoid after learning more about them.

There is no completely safe sweetener - all have drawbacks or side effects. While honey or maple syrup, used in small amounts, are better than refined sugars, fruit juices are probably the best choice for sweeteners.

Polydextrose

Artificial sweeteners do not add bulk to a product, only sweetness. This is a problem in the manufacture of frozen desserts, instant puddings, cakes, and hard candies. Polydextrose is a bulking agent consisting of dextrose, sorbitol, and citric acid. It is a suitable replacement for sucrose, carbohydrates, and fats in many food products; however, the sorbitol content of polydextrose can cause a laxative effect if more than 50 grams a day are consumed.

Aspartame

Aspartame is about 200 times sweeter than sucrose and can intensify the taste of other flavours and sweeteners. It cannot be used in heated products, however, since high temperatures cause aspartame to break down. It also loses its sweetness after long storage.

Aspartame is composed of two amino acids, phenylalanine and aspartic acid, which are linked together with a molecule of methanol. When aspartame is broken down in our bodies, this molecule of methanol is released by the small intestine into the bloodstream. The methanol is converted to formaldehyde and is further degraded. In sufficient amounts, methanol and formaldehyde can cause neurological damage, eye damage, or blindness. The phenylalanine in aspartame is not safe for those with phenylketonuria (the inability to oxidize a metabolic product of phenylalanine). **Taking large amounts of aspartame over time can upset the amino acid and neurotransmitter balance in our bodies.**

Among the reported symptoms of side effects after aspartame use are: headaches, dizziness, confusion, depression, blindness, tinnitus (ringing in the ears), nausea, diarrhea, frequent urination, tremors, abdominal pain, shortness of breath, chest pain, convulsions, and slurring of speech.

Mannitol

Mannitol is found in many plants and plant extracts, but is usually derived from seaweed. Mannitol is poorly digested by our body, and in relatively small amounts can cause diarrhea. In intravenous feedings, it has been associated with a wide range of problems. Mannitol can also induce, or worsen, kidney diseases. It leaves a cool sweet taste in the mouth and is used in:

- Antacid tablets
- Breath fresheners
- Chewing gum
- Children's aspirin tablets
- Cough and cold tablets

- Sugarless candies

Xylitol

Xylitol is made from xylose, a wood sugar. It can also be obtained from corn cobs, peanut shells, wheat straw, cotton seed hulls, and coconut shells. Xylitol has the same sweetness as sucrose and leaves a pleasant, cool taste in the mouth, but can cause diarrhea if consumed at high levels. Intravenous xylitol infusions have been prohibited in other countries, and tests of this material have produced some alarming results. In North American, it is still used in the manufacturing of chewing gum.

SUGAR AND ALL THINGS SWEET

North American has turned into a land of "sugarholics". The average North American consumes approximately his or her own weight in sugar per year; the national average being over 130 pounds of sugar per person. This amount consists of the refined sugar added to foods we choose to eat, in addition to the naturally occurring sugars in fruits and vegetables. Much of the sugar we eat is "hidden" sugar. Foods that were once unsweetened are now sweetened, and others that previously were sweet, have been elevated to higher levels of sweetness.

Hidden sugars are largely the result of industrial practices that are largely unfamiliar to the public. For example, sugar content of meat is increased by feeding it to animals before slaughter to improve the flavour and colour of the meat, and by adding it to the meat itself as it is prepared in packing houses and restaurants. Any dish prepared with ground meat may contain added syrups, to help minimize shrinkage and to improve flavour, juiciness, and texture.

The presence of hidden sugars should be suspected in the following items, either because the manufacturers are not required to list the sugar content, or because the sugars are listed in such a fashion that the consumer does not recognize them as sugars.

- Bouillon cubes
- Breading for fried or baked poultry and meats
- Canned and frozen vegetables

- Ketchup
- Cigarettes
- Convenience foods
- Cottage cheese
- Dry roasted nuts
- Frozen and canned entrees
- Gravies
- Instant coffee
- Instant tea
- Iodized salt
- Luncheon meats
- Mixes to stretch chopped beef
- Peanut butter
- Potato chips
- Salad dressings
- Soups
- Wieners

When sugar is listed, the exact percentage is difficult to determine. Sugar appears on labels under many names; the 'ose' ending of words indicates a sugar. All of the following items are sugars:

- Brown sugar
- Corn syrup
- Corn syrup solids
- Dextrose
- Fructose
- Glucose
- High-fructose corn syrup
- Honey
- Malt syrup
- Maltodextrin
- Mannitol
- Maple syrup
- Molasses
- Raw sugar
- Sorbitol

- Sorghum
- Sucrose
- Turbinado
- Xylitol

Sugar, like alcohol, is rapidly absorbed and floods the system, predisposing the sensitive person to severe reactions and addictions. High sugar intake has been linked to dental cavities, obesity, diabetes, coronary heart disease, and hypoglycemia and behaviour problems. Too much sugar depletes the body of specific nutrients, including the B vitamins, magnesium, chromium, manganese, and other minerals.

Our body machinery is designed to cope with about 2 teaspoons of sugar per day. If we eat additional amounts of sugar - such as a piece of apple pie, with 19 teaspoons for sugar - it disrupts our body's "sugar equilibrium". These disruptions stress our body and overload the adrenal glands and pancreas, which are critical to allergy control.

Children should not be given sweets on an empty stomach. Young children eat small amounts of food, and are dependent on this food to obtain the nutrients they need. Eating sugar, which has little nutritional value, adversely affects their appetites, thus decreasing their intake of nutrients. Try not to use sweets as a reward.

The following sweeteners are commonly used in North America: sucrose, corn sweeteners, dextrose, and glucose.

Sucrose

Sucrose is the most commonly used sugar in our food supply. It can be refined from both sugar cane and sugar beets, and the resulting sugars have identical structures, however, many hypersensitive people can distinguish one from the other by their reaction to the small residues of the source plants.

Sucrose stimulates the production of fat in the body, particularly in women using contraceptive drugs.

Beet and Cane sugars are used as:

- Fermentation mediums in baked goods contributing to the colour, flavour, and quality of the crust, retention of moisture, and extension of shelf life
- Curing agents for processed meats
- Preservatives in fruits, jellies, jams and preserves
- Bulking agents in ice cream, baked goods and confections
- Preservatives in medications
- Ointments

Remember: Whatever you put into, or onto, your body eventually gets into your bloodstream

Corn Sweeteners

Over half of the cornstarch milled in North America is used to produce corn sweeteners. They are used extensively by the food industry because of their low cost, and because a sweeter mix is obtained when they are combined with sucrose.

Corn sugar carries all of the allergenicity of corn, and many corn sensitive people react to it more quickly than other components of corn. As the food industry has stepped up its use of corn sweeteners and cornstarch, sensitivities to corn have risen. **Corn-sensitive people must avoid product containing dextrose, glucose, sorbitol and mannitol.**

Corn sugar found in infant formulas can produce eczema and gastrointestinal upsets in corn-sensitive babies, and diarrhea in all infants.

Corn Sweeteners:
- Add body and texture to soft drinks
- Add "chewiness" to confections and chewing gums
- Are used in maple, nut and root beer flavouring for beverages, ice cream candy and baked goods.
- Are used in processed meats, hams, bacon, fish products, and sausages
- Help retain bright colours in preserves, cured meats, and ketchup
- Absorb moisture to keep hard candy from becoming sticky

- Inhibit crystallization of other sugars
- Ferment easily which aids brewers and distillers

Dextrose

Dextrose, maltose, corn syrup, and corn sugar are derivatives of cornstarch. Dextrose, in addition to the uses listed above, is an ingredient in intravenous solutions commonly used in hospitals.

Glucose

Glucose is commercially processed sugar derived from cornstarch, occurring naturally in grapes and corn. Its name can be misleading since blood sugar is also referred to as glucose. It is frequently labeled a corn syrup because the public at one time thought it was a sugar derived from glue.

Glucose is a dangerous sweetener because of its low sweetness level. It is only 1/5 as sweet as sucrose. Therefore, large quantities can be absorbed without a person being aware of its presence in food. It is frequently used to flavour ground meat dishes, luncheon meats, and hams, as well as to extend maple syrup.

The following information about milk should explain why you may wish to eliminate it from the diet.

Milk

The major components of milk are: lactalbumin, casein, lactose (milk sugar) and cream. It is the lactalbumin component that varies from species to species. For example, the lactalbumin of human milk is different from that of cow's milk, and both are different from the lactalbumin of goat's milk. For this reason, some people who react allergically to cow's milk may be able to drink goat's milk without difficulty. People who are sensitive to all components of milk will be unable to tolerate milk from any animal source. Any product containing milk by-products or milk proteins and sugars, will cause the same symptoms as milk and should be avoided.

Watch for these ingredients when reading product labels or checking contents of food served to you: butter, cream, butterfat, whipped cream, skim milk, powdered milk, condensed milk, evaporated milk, milk solids, whey, yoghurt, casein, casein ate, non-fat milk solids or lactalbumin. Since milk is pasteurized twice before delivery to market, all of the 'live' enzymes have been destroyed. A 'dead' food provides minimal or no nutritional value because the body's enzymes cannot break it down.

Food Sources of Milk

☐ Au gratin dishes	☐ Baby foods	☐ Baked goods
☐ Batters	☐ Butter	☐ Buttermilk
☐ Cakes	☐ Carob coatings	☐ Canned milk
☐ Carob chips	☐ Chocolate beverages	☐ Casein
☐ Cheeses	☐ Condensed milk	☐ Chocolate creams
☐ Cocomalt	☐ Cream	☐ Cookies
☐ Cottage cheese	☐ Curds	☐ Cream sauces
☐ Creamed soups	☐ Dried milk	☐ Custard
☐ Doughnuts	☐ Flours (i.e. Bisquick)	☐ Evaporated milk
☐ Filled candy bars	☐ Hot cereals (some)	☐ Fritters
☐ Gravies	☐ Ice milk	☐ Hot dogs
☐ Ice cream	☐ Lactate	☐ Kefir
☐ Latalbumin	☐ Malted milk	☐ Lacto globulin
☐ Lactose	☐ Milk puddings	☐ Margarine
☐ Milk chocolate candy	☐ Omelets	☐ Non-dairy products
☐ Nougat candy	☐ Powdered milk	☐ Ovaltine ™
☐ Pancakes	☐ Salad dressings	☐ Pudding mixes

☐ Rarebits	☐ Skim milk	☐ Sausages
☐ Sherbet	☐ Sour cream	☐ Stroganoff
☐ Soufflés	☐ Waffles	☐ Whey
☐ Whipped cream	☐ Wiener schnitzel	☐ Yoghurt

Problems with Milk

Many people have difficulty drinking milk because it contains lactose (known as milk sugar), and the enzyme lactase is needed to digest the lactose. Many children gradually lose the lactase enzyme, usually between the ages of one and four, and are no longer able to digest milk sugar.

Cow's milk is a common food allergen, and people may therefore be sensitive to all milk components. Symptoms of this allergy include: vomiting, diarrhea, bloody diarrhea, asthma, runny or stuffy nose, recurrent ear infections, rashes, hives, and hyperactive behaviour. Studies have linked delinquency and behaviour disorders to high milk intake. Infant colic is related to cow's milk formula, or milk that a breast feeding mother may be drinking.

EXCESS PROTEIN

The average North American eats 80-125 grams of protein per day. Reference books indicate the recommended daily intake of 30-55 grams of protein is all that is necessary. Less is more, because the body re-uses amino acids to economize protein metabolism.

Protein Count for Food Sources:

4 oz broiled chicken	33 g protein
4 oz. broiled fresh flounder	27g protein
2 slices pepperoni pizza	26 g protein
4 oz. almonds	20 g protein
1 egg	6 g protein
½ cup kidney beans	6 g protein

Protein is absolutely essential for health. It is **excess** protein that creates problems.

Please remember the following:

Beef is a good source of protein and certain vitamins however, only small amounts are needed in order to supply the essential nutrients.

Natural Sources of Calcium

Many parents and adults often wonder how they can receive the optimal intake of calcium if they are eliminating milk and milk products from their diets. The following list should provide you with some good alternatives:

Seeds and Nuts

    Sesame seeds are very high in calcium   (1 cup = 2200 mg calcium)

    Almonds   (1 cup = 600 mg calcium)

    Filberts   (1 cup = 424 mg calcium)

    Sunflower seeds   (1 cup = 260 mg calcium

    Walnuts   (1 cup =216 mg calcium)

Nut Butters - *not peanut butter as it is very allergenic and contains the least amount of calcium.*

    Sesame butter   (3 oz = 843 mg calcium)

    Almond butter   (3 oz = 225 mg calcium)

Vegetables

    ½ cup turnip greens   (53 mg calcium)

    ½ cup green beans   (22 mg calcium)

    ½ cup broccoli   (21 mg calcium)

    1 medium carrot   (19 mg calcium)

    ½ cup cabbage   (18 mg calcium)

    ½ cup spinach   (16 mg calcium)

Beans and Rice

Soybeans	(1 cup = 460 mg calcium)
Tofu	(1 cup = 258 mg calcium)
Navy beans	(1 cup = 128 mg calcium)
3 bean salad	(1 cup = 88 mg calcium)
Pinto beans	(1 cup = 82 mg calcium)
Chick peas	(1 cup = 80 mg calcium)
Kidney beans	(1 cup = 50 mg calcium)
Wild rice	(1 cup = 30 mg calcium)
Brown rice	(1 cup = 23 mg calcium)

Fish

Sardines	(3 oz. = 375 mg calcium)
Salmon	(3 oz. = 203 mg calcium)

Ways in which calcium may be lost from the body:

- Coffee, tea, soda pop and chocolate: Intake of caffeine causes increased calcium loss in the urine.
- Refined sugar: Ingestion of sugar increases calcium loss through urine. When foods containing calcium are taken with sugar, the absorption of usable calcium through the intestine is greatly reduced. Most junk foods are a high source of sugar.
- Phosphorus: Soft drinks have high phosphorus content. Phosphorus binds with calcium, therefore, when phosphorus is high in the blood, it can pull calcium from the bones contributing to a calcium deficiency.

Nutritional Supplementation

Nutritional supplementation is the addition of vitamins, minerals and oils to the diet to assist healthy maintenance of the body. Vitamins and minerals are micro nutrients needed for the body's normal growth, function and health. The body cannot make most micronutrients so we must get them from foods we eat, or in some cases, from dietary supplements.

The students in my research group were taken off all medication and were then given only fresh food cooked daily by the resident chef. No junk food was allowed for 6 weeks and, after that, the chef provided some form of healthy dessert once a week. Establishing a healthy diet is important. Whole foods like fruits and vegetables are essential. Fish, lean proteins, fiber and some dairy, if your child is not allergic, are necessary for optimal health. Eating a variety of fruits and vegetables will help maximize nutrient intake. Taking a supplement can fill the nutrient gaps. The current thought is that a whole food, green formula, versus an encapsulated multivitamin is preferred. Consult a homeopathic doctor for advice.

It is widely known that many modern illnesses are linked to vitamin and nutrient deficiencies which cause molecular imbalances leading to problems. None of the students in my research group received any supplements as the school's focus was to provide a healthy, balanced diet, daily exercise, a structured learning environment, minimal exposure to television and a regular sleep routine.

The program I designed to help children diagnosed with ADHD is based on medical research of the 1980's and 1990's. Prior to teaching about my research and the program to eliminate the symptoms of ADHD on a grand scale, I accepted children of local families and children referred to me by close-at-hand school boards and doctors, so as to closely monitor the children's progress. This also provided insight about the benefits of supplementation.

INSTRUCTIONS FOR SUPPLEMENTATION

1. Purchase a multivitamin complex that contains vitamins A.B.C.E., zinc, selenium, calcium and magnesium and potassium. If you cannot find one that contains all eight ingredients, purchase them in whatever combination recommended. For children under 12, most of my clients have found Nubears™ or Good Friends™ to be easily taken.

2. The Essential Fatty Acids come in three forms: liquid, gel capsule, and seeds. My clients have found gel caps and liquid the easiest to administer. If your child is too young to swallow these capsules, or suffers from gagging, simply pierce the capsule and rub the oil along the jaw bone, or on the belly. It will be absorbed. One-half teaspoon daily is all that is necessary for children under 12. As always, read and follow label instructions.

3. Plant enzymes should be taken before each meal. If your child suffers from allergies or bedwetting, taking a plant enzyme before bedtime seems to increase the healing process.

4. If you, or your child, have taken antibiotics frequently, then it is likely advisable to purchase LACTOBACILLUS ACIDOPHILUS to replenish the intestinal "friendly" bacteria. There are many companies selling 'friendly bacteria'. Ask questions and purchase the most pure. Pro-biotics, as compared to anti-biotics, is the approach favoured for the future.

A word of caution regarding supplements

As always, one must follow the directions on the package or bottle in consultation with a health care professional. If a problem arises, it is wise to seek medical assistance. No synthetic vitamin program should be followed for more that 9-12 months without changing the brand. All vitamins should be pure, natural and without preservatives, colours or fillers.

REMEMBER: THERE IS NO "PILL" SOLUTION FOR BAD HABITS

Nutrient Therapy

Nutrient therapy, also known as orthomolecular therapy, means supplying the cells with the right mixture of nutrients. Many diseases are known to be the result of the wrong balance of essential nutrients in the body. Adjusting the diet, eliminating junk foods, and ingesting the proper doses of essential vitamins, minerals and amino acids, can correct the chemical imbalance of disease and disorders.

The nutrient therapy approach helps us become more aware of the dangerously polluted environment in which we live and about the nutrient-stripped refined foods most of us eat. The nutrient approach is both corrective and preventive.

Nutrient therapy takes into account that every individual is biochemically unique. Every person has a very different nutrient and amino acid requirement. Through the process of orthomolecular therapy, the mind and body can achieve a state of homeostasis - a condition where everything in the body is in balance and capable of resisting environmental changes, while regulating internal metabolic function. Every tissue of the body is affected by nutrition. Under conditions of poor nutrition, the kidneys stop filtering, the stomach stops digesting, the adrenals stop secreting, and the other organs follow suit.

A child's state of health is his/her state of nutrition. When minerals, vitamins, amino acids, enzymes or even hormones are deficient, the result can be a disturbed biochemical balance causing impaired functions in the brain.

Experts state that Ritalin™ is a potent stimulant available only by a physician's prescription. The prescription rates for Ritalin™ have continued to climb. The U.S. drug enforcement administration lists five grades of controlled substances based on abuse potential. Heroin and LSD are "Schedule 1" drugs. "Schedule 2" drugs include morphine, opium and Ritalin™ and yet this potent drug is being used as a quick fix to quiet or calm children.

Children who show signs of hyperkinesis, hyperactivity or ADHD could have an imbalance in their biochemistry. An untreated biochemical imbalance can cause a child to display hyperactive behaviour and may result in physical illness as well.

Hyperactivity is a major problem facing parents and teachers. While children who are hyperactive may also exhibit behaviour problems, behaviour modification techniques appear to have little or no long term effects. These behaviour problems often result in a child being labeled as willful, aggressive, impulsive, and a disruptive influence in the home and at school. Not all children who are hyperactive are aggressive. Some are very passive, withdrawn and find it difficult to communicate their feelings.

Hyperactivity is not a condition that can be measured in precise scientific terms. Nor is it a situation that has a quick fix, especially with a powerful and addictive drug such as Ritalin ™. Hyperactivity is a behavioural complex in which the child demonstrates maladaptive or disorganized behaviour characteristics, which put him out of sync with the world around him. Hyperactive children are extremely vulnerable to other people and to their own inadequacies. Having said this, I believe that my research and drug-free program will help you, and your child, eliminate hyperactive behaviour and lead a 'normal' life according to ability and attitude.

THE TREATMENT OF HYPERACTIVITY WITH NUTRIENTS

We often do not realize the body's need for nutrients because we do not realize how busy the human body is, even small ones. A nutrient is different from a drug. A nutrient is a food substance that in most cases supplies the energy for the molecular building blocks or processes the body requires.

Consider these facts:

- A human has the equivalent of a new skin every 24 days
- Most of the white blood cells are replaced every 10 days
- Every second the bone marrow makes 2.5 million red blood cells
- Every 4 days most of the lining of the gastro-intestinal tract and the blood platelets are replaced.

What do these supplements do? Where are they found?

Socrates once said, "There is only one good - knowledge; and one evil -- ignorance." This very important statement should guide all of us when it comes to making decisions about our health. When illness occurs, we rely on physicians to cure us. What many fail to realize is that the cure is within each one of us. Nature has provided us with a wondrous immune system and all we have to do is take proper care of this inner healing force.

When taking supplements to help the body's immune system, it is advisable to take the recommended dosages. If you experience an allergic reaction to any supplement, immediately discontinue its use. Recent research indicates that we should be replenishing our bodies with essential nutrients, as our food sources are not able to meet all of our needs. Additionally, we need to fortify and strengthen our systems so that they can deal with an ever increasingly polluted environment. It is always advisable to receive the advice of a medical doctor or trained health care professional.

"Supernutrition" involves a complete chain of some 40 nutrients, including:
- Vitamins
- Minerals
- Trace elements
- Amino acids
- Enzymes

Every nutrient in the following list acts like a gear in a complicated machine. There are no nutrients which are totally independent or dispensable in the human machine.

Vitamin A - plays a vital role in the production and integrity of epithelial cells (skin, inner linings); immune system booster; antioxidant properties

> **Sources:** fish liver oils, animal livers, green and yellow fruits and vegetables, pumpkin, yellow squash, turnip greens, watercress, spinach, sweet potatoes, red peppers, peaches, parsley, dandelion, Swiss chard, beets, apricots, asparagus, garlic, mustard

Vitamin B_1 (Thiamine) - essential for carbohydrate metabolism; antioxidant properties; requirements increase during times of stress

> **Sources**: brown rice, fish, organ meat, peanuts, peas, pork, poultry, rice, bran, soybeans, wheat germ, whole grains, oatmeal, plums, dried prunes, raisins, beans, brussel sprouts, broccoli

Vitamin B_2 (Riboflavin) - vital for healthy blood and tissue repair; requirements increase during times of stress

> **Sources**: beans, cheese, eggs, fish, meat milk, poultry, spinach, yoghurt, currants, nuts, brussel sprouts, avocados, broccoli

Vitamin B_3 (Niacin and Niacinamide) - vital for proper circulation and healthy skin; aids in the functioning of the nervous system, and the metabolism of carbohydrates, fats and proteins

> **Sources**: beef, broccoli, carrots, cheese, corn flour, eggs, fish, milk, pork potatoes, tomatoes, whole wheat

Vitamin B_5 (Pantothenic Acid) - anti-stress vitamin helps in the production of adrenal hormones, and the formation of antibodies, aids in vitamin utilization and helps to convert fats, carbohydrates and proteins into energy

> **Sources**: beans, beef, eggs, salt-water fish, mother's milk, pork fresh vegetables, whole wheat

Vitamin B$_6$ (Pyridoxine) - is involved in more bodily functions than any other single nutrient; affects both physical and mental health; helpful in the treatment of allergies and asthma

> **Sources**: All foods contain traces of vitamin B6 but these foods have the highest amounts: brewer's yeast, carrots, chicken, eggs, fish, meat, peas spinach, sunflower seeds, walnuts, wheat germ, bananas, beans, brown rice, cabbage and cantaloupe

Vitamin B$_{12}$ (Cobalamin) - needed to promote normal growth and development; prevents nerve damage; needed to prevent anemia; required for the proper digestion and absorption of foods, protein synthesis and metabolism of carbohydrates and fats

> **Sources**: blue cheese, cheese, clams, herring, kidney, liver, mackerel, milk, seafood, tofu, red meat; Vitamin B$_{12}$ is not found in vegetables; it is only available from animal sources

Biotin - aids in cell growth, fatty acid production, and in the metabolism of carbohydrates, fats and proteins; facilitates the utilization of the B-complex vitamins; sufficient quantities are needed for healthy hair and skin

> **Sources**: egg yolk, salt-water fish, meat, milk, poultry, soybeans, whole grains, yeast

Choline - vital for nerve transmission, gallbladder regulation, liver function and lecithin formation; minimizes excess fat in the liver; without choline, brain function and memory are impaired

> **Sources**: egg yolks, legumes, meat, milk; whole grain cereals (not processed cereals)

Folic Acid - needed for energy production and the formation of red blood cells; helps regulate embryonic and fetal development of nerve cells; vital for normal growth and development; works best when combined with Vitamin B$_{12}$

> **Sources**: barley, beans, beef, bran, brewer's yeast, brown rice, cheese, chicken, dates, green leafy vegetables,

lamb, lentils, milk, oranges, organ meats, split peas, pork, root vegetables, salmon, tuna, wheat germ, whole grains, whole wheat, yeast

Vitamin C - antioxidant properties, required for tissue growth and repair, adrenal gland function and healthy gums; protects against the harmful effects of pollution, is thought to prevent cancer, protect against infections and enhance immunity; protects against bruising; promotes the healing of wounds and the production of anti-stress hormones; has been found to work well with Vitamin E, and the combined effect is greater than the two vitamins working alone.

> **Sources**: asparagus, avocados, beet greens, broccoli, brussel sprouts, cantaloupe, collard greens, currents, grapefruit, kale, lemons, mangoes, mustard greens, onions, oranges, papaya, parsley, green peas, sweet peppers, persimmons, pineapple, radishes, rose hips, spinach, strawberries, Swiss chard, tomatoes, turnip greens and watercress

Ester C (polyascorbate) - a breakthrough in Vitamin C technology because it enters the bloodstream and tissues 4 times faster and gets into the blood cells more efficiently

Vitamin D - required for calcium and phosphorus absorption and utilization; necessary for growth and is especially important for normal growth and development of bones and teeth in children; enhances immunity; can be synthesized in the body by exposing the skin to sunlight

> **Sources**: fish liver oils, fatty salt-water fish, dairy products fortified with vitamin D, eggs; found in alfalfa, butter, cod liver oil, egg yolk, halibut liver, milk oatmeal, salmon, sardines, sweet potatoes, tuna and vegetable oils

Vitamin E - antioxidant properties, anti-carcinogenic properties; thought to prevent cancer and cardiovascular disease; promotes normal clotting and healing; reduces scarring; reduces blood pressure, reduces severity of leg cramps; the body needs zinc in order to maintain the proper levels of Vitamin E in the blood

>**Sources**: cold-pressed vegetable oils, whole grains, dark green leafy vegetables, nuts, seeds, legumes, brown rice, cornmeal, eggs, oatmeal, milk, liver, organ meats, potatoes and wheat germ

Vitamin K - created by the bacteria in the intestine; needed for blood clotting; may play a role in bone formation.

>**Sources**: alfalfa, broccoli, dark green leafy vegetables, soybeans, blackstrap molasses, brussel sprouts, cabbage, cauliflower, egg yolks, liver, oatmeal, oats, rye, safflower oil and wheat

Bioflavonoid - not true vitamins; antioxidant properties; potent anti-inflammatory properties; strengthens capillary walls and prevents capillary damage; sometimes referred to as Vitamin P; enhances absorption of Vitamin C when taken together. The body cannot produce bioflavonoids

>**Sources**: white material just beneath the peel of citrus fruits, peppers, buckwheat, black currants, apricots, cherries, grapefruit, grapes, lemons, oranges, prunes, rose hips

Quercetin - found in blue-green algae and available as a supplement; may effectively treat and prevent asthma symptoms

Coenzyme Q-10 - very important vitamin-like substance that resembles Vitamin E; powerful antioxidant; also called a ubiquinone; found in human tissue; plays a crucial role in the effectiveness of the immune system and in the aging process; because it declines with our age, it should be supplemented in the diet.

>**Sources**: beef heart, spinach, mackerel, salmon, sardines, peanuts

Zinc - required for protein synthesis; promotes healthy immune system
> **Sources**: egg yolk, seafood, liver, legumes, soy
> products

Selenium - inhibits the oxidation of lipids (fats); a powerful antioxidant, particularly when combined with Vitamin E
> **Sources**: brown rice, broccoli, poultry, seafood, liver,
> whole grains, sea vegetables

Calcium - activates enzymes involved in fat and protein digestion and in the production of energy; involved in blood clotting and the transmission of nerve impulses; important for cardiovascular functions
> **Sources**: dairy products, canned salmon and sardines
> (including the bones); green leafy vegetables such as
> collard, turnip and mustard greens, clams, oysters,
> shrimp, kale, broccoli, soy products

Magnesium - maintains the function of nerves, essential to enzyme activity and cardiovascular function; works with calcium to contract and relax the muscles
> **Sources:** dairy products, meat, fish and seafood, nuts,
> blackstrap molasses, soy products, wheat germ, seeds
> peanuts, oatmeal, rice, cornmeal

Plant Enzymes - energized protein molecules - play important role in virtually all biochemical activities that occur in the body; ensures proper digestion of food
> **Sources**: avocados, papayas, pineapple, bananas,
> mangos; most commercially available enzyme products
> are made from animal enzymes

Essential Fatty Acids - necessary for the formation and proper balance of prostaglandins (responsible for every system and function in the body) - oils regulate vital metabolic processes throughout the body.

Two fatty acids considered essential to life are: Omega 3 and Omega 6

> **Omega 3 sources:** cold -weather plants (primarily bean oils, canola, and flaxseed oils) and animals (primarily cold water fatty fish such as: salmon, cod, mackerel, and tuna)
>
> **Omega 6 Sources:** very little found in common foods, evening primrose oil, borage oil, and black current oil are more dependable sources

Echinacea - derived from the purple coneflower plant; and herb known for its immune system boosting properties; its available in tincture or capsule form

SUPPLEMENTATION PROGRAM

Listed below are the recommended supplements found to be very beneficial in helping to eliminate the symptoms associated with ADHD.

* Multiple Vitamin (A, B, C, E, Zinc, Selenium, Calcium, Magnesium, Potassium)
* Essential Fatty Acid (flaxseed, evening primrose or cod liver oil)
* Digestive Enzymes
* Acidophilus or probiotic to restore balance in intestines.

OPTIMUM DAILY ALLOWANCE FOR VITAMINS AND MINERALS

Please note:
The following information has been compiled from a variety of sources and is based on research reported in over 65 medical journals, including <u>Nutrition Research</u>, <u>Journal of Medical Science</u>, <u>British Journal of Dermatology</u>, and <u>Journal of Clinical Nutrition</u>.

Vitamin A:

        10,000 - 50,000 IU per day - no known toxicity
        50,000 - 100,000 IU per day for the following conditions: allergies, asthma, dry skin, acne, eczema, and sinusitis - no known toxicity
*Pregnant women or nursing mothers should consult their physicians

Vitamin B:

> B$_1$ Thiamin 25-300 mg - no known toxicity
>
> B$_2$ Riboflavin 50-300 mg - no known toxicity
>
> B$_3$ Niacin and Niacinamide 25-300 mg no known toxicity; however flushing may occur
>
> B$_5$ Pantothenic Acid 25-300 mg - no known toxicity
>
> B$_6$ 25-300 mg for asthma; 50-300 mg - relatively non toxic but some side effects noted at doses of 2,000-6,000 mg per day
>
> B$_{12}$ 25-300 mcg for anxiety or depression; 100-500 mcg - no known toxicity

Vitamin C:

> 500-5,000 mg along with 500-5,000 mg *bioflavonoid
>
> No proven toxicity for vitamin C
>
> Allergies or asthma: 3,000-5,000 mg
>
> Enhanced immunity: 1,000-5,000 mg
>
> Exposure to cigarette smoke and polluted air: 1,000-5,000 mg
>
> *Grapeseed extract or Pycnogenol are 2 well-known bioflavonoids. Many vitamin supplements contain bioflavonoid.

Vitamin E:

> 200-800 IU per day; toxicity noted above 1,000 IU per day

Omega 3:

> No optimum dosage for Omega 3 fatty acids
>
> Flaxseed oil (follow directions on bottle)
>
> No known toxicity

Omega 6:

> No optimum dosage for Omega 6 fatty acids
>
> Evening Primrose Oil (1-6 capsules daily)
>
> Borage (1 capsule daily)
>
> No known toxic effects

Selenium:

> 100-400 mcg per day
>
> No known toxicity at these levels.
>
> (Most absorbable, and least toxic, comes from ocean plants or selenium rich yeast)

Zinc:

> 22.5-50 mg
>
> No known toxicity at these levels

> DO NOT STOP TAKING VITAMINS AND MINERALS ABRUPTLY. CONSULT WITH A HEALTH CARE PROFESSIONAL FOR ADVICE

ADDITIONAL INFORMATION

- Our bodies need many more minerals for good health than plants do for growth. Humans must get minerals from external sources.
- Safflower, sunflower, and soy, are natural fats designed to do life-supporting work in the body.
- B$_6$ is an immune system booster. It is an important vitamin for the conversion of food to energy. Vitamin B$_6$ is a precursor to at least 50 enzymes and is needed for the metabolism of all amino acids. Enzymes are built from amino acids, which makes vitamin B$_6$ a very essential part of enzyme production.
- Magnesium is the mineral in greatest demand; it is needed for enzyme production.
- The mineral potassium is essential for every cell in the body. A severe deficiency will cause the heart to stop beating.
- Experts all agree that milk is the number one allergen. Medical textbooks on pediatrics also acknowledge the allergencity of milk to babies and children. It should be noted that calcium is no more or less important than some other minerals.
- Beta Carotene assists vitamin A production in the body, and may be taken instead of vitamin A.
- Vitamin C is an antioxidant, aids in tissue repair and growth, enhances immunity, supports the adrenal glands, and helps promote healthy gums.

- <u>Zinc is an immune system booster</u>. It plays an important role in cell division and repair, is good for wound healing and assists in promoting normal sight, taste, and smell. As a key ingredient of enzymes, it helps facilitate vital chemical actions. Zinc is essential for processing carbohydrate foods.
- <u>Kelp</u> is rich in all trace minerals, particularly iodine.
- <u>Selenium</u> is an antioxidant that slows aging. Selenium and vitamin E form a powerful healing partnership. Together they help fight and conquer illness and can mitigate the toxicity of cadmium found in auto exhaust and cigarette smoke.
- Excess protein depletes calcium from the body. High protein consumption contributes more to the depletion of calcium from bones than does a deficiency of calcium intake.
- Essential fatty acid deficiency is probably the most common, but least recognized, nutritional deficiency which leads to immune system breakdown, setting the stage for allergy. Children are especially dependent upon essential fatty acids for brain development.
- People experiencing essential fatty acid deficiency are prone to allergies, sinus problems, hay fever, asthma, eczema, PMS, etc.. Some symptoms indicative of the deficiency are:
  - Bleeding gums
  - Excess ear wax
  - Cold hands and feet
  - Dry brittle or oily hair
  - Dry flaky skin
  - Lowered resistance to infection
- Lifestyle habits that may create a fatty acid deficiency are:
  - High intake of refined sugar
  - Excess intake of saturated fat
  - High consumption of fried foods
  - Drug usage and overuse of antibiotics
- Natural foods containing essential fatty acids are:
  - Raw, unsalted nuts
  - Raw unsalted seeds (e.g. pumpkin, sunflower, sesame, and flax)
  - Beans
  - Avocado

- Green leafy vegetables
- Cold water fish
- Commercially sold safflower oil has been refined, and therefore its Omega 6 (Evening Primrose Oil) content has been virtually destroyed in the manufacturing process.
- To help your child recover from infections:
  - Give lactobacillus acidophilus or a 'total flora' product which can be purchased in a health food store. These help support the functioning of the immune system by aiding in resistance to infections.

Tryptophan, an essential amino acid, is necessary to maintain the body in protein balance. It has a variety of important roles in mental activity. **Serotonin** is a neurotransmitter, one of the chemicals in the brain that helps control moods. To have enough serotonin you need enough tryptophan which is essential in its formation. B_6 (pyridoxine) is needed to form serotonin. Many hyperactive children have low serotonin, tryptophan, and B_6 levels. Tryptophan raises the low levels of blood serotonin. Supplements containing tryptophan and B_6 can correct some of the biochemical disorders related to aggression. A few years ago, tryptophan was wrongly implicated in the deaths of some individuals taking it. For this reason, it has been removed from supplements. It is however, found in a variety of foods such as turkey.

The anxiety and stress of a hyperactive child is stored in the limbic system, the emotional part of the brain. Under prolonged periods of stress, the limbic system releases the anxiety-related messages. It fires at the cortex, or the "thinking part" of the brain, and the child becomes overwhelmed. The result is either hyper-aggressive or hyper-passive behaviours. The child has no control over the behaviour.

Magnesium is commonly deficient in hyperactive people. Magnesium has a quieting effect on the central nervous system. When it is added to the hyperactive person's diet, calming effects are sometimes seen immediately. Magnesium has been used as a nervous system sedative. Magnesium, along with **calcium**, is a sedative-type of mineral. Symptoms of magnesium deficiency include: apprehension, nervous irritability, muscle twitch, tremors, noise sensitivity, confusion, and disorientation.

Calcium is a strong countering agent against lead. Children with inadequate calcium in their diets appear to be more likely to get lead intoxication. A child who is found to be sensitive to dairy products is not likely to be receiving proper amounts of dietary calcium. Since dairy products are a major food source of calcium, it may be necessary to supplement this mineral. A calcium deficiency may also induce hyperactivity. The calcium deficient child may be: irritable, sleep disturbed, angry, and inattentive. These symptoms may improve dramatically when the calcium needs are met. The first signs of a calcium deficiency are: nervous stomach, cramps, and tingling in the arms and legs.

The very first signs of vitamin B deficiency appear in the psychological category. The symptoms are: fear, depression, temper tantrums, anxiety, mood swings, inability to concentrate, withdrawal, listlessness, and a general feeling of fatigue. Often children with behaviour disorders have chronic, marginal B deficiencies. The signals of the B deficiency include: aggressive personality changes, sleep problems, recurring bad dreams, and heightened anxiety.

Niacinamide (B_3) is another vitamin that offers help for the hyperactive child. It seems to have a settling influence on a distractible child, and the quieting effect on the central nervous system. Vitamins B_5 and B_6 are also important.

Vitamin C is considered by some to be the most important vitamin in the treatment of hyperactivity. Vitamin C given on a daily basis is thought to be the most inexpensive nutritional insurance policy for your child's health.

Nutritional Deficiencies

Please note the various symptoms of nutritional deficiencies and how they may apply to yourself or your child.

Vitamin A Deficiency
(Symptoms)

- Acne, especially upper back and upper arms
- Night blindness
- Growth impairment
- Dry skin
- Poor coordination
- Dry mouth
- Chronic diarrhea
- Scaly patches of skin

Vitamin B$_6$ Deficiency
(Symptoms)

- Fluid retention
- Heart problems
- Night time cramps
- Poor concentration
- Bad breath
- Oily hair
- Convulsions
- Short-term memory loss

- Sensitivity to MSG (monosodium glutamate)
- Autism
- Depression
- Acne
- Mood swings
- Sleeping problems
- Dry patches of skin on face
- Tendency to cry easily
- Lack of dreams

Vitamin B$_{12}$ Deficiency
(Symptoms)

- Dark circles under eyes
- Chronic fatigue
- Chronic constipation
- Memory loss
- Paranoia
- Pale complexion
- Depression
- Nervousness
- Loss of balance
- Numbness in hands, feet, legs
- Loss of taste

Mineral Deficiencies
Calcium
(Symptoms)

- Brittle nails
- Chronic head aches
- Soft teeth
- Leg cramps
- Nose bleeds
- ADHD
- Joint pain
- Slow pulse rate

- Anxiety
- Nervousness
- Irritability

Magnesium
(Symptoms)

- Chronic fatigue
- Depression
- Inability to control bladder
- Night sweats
- Excessive body odour
- Muscle twitching
- Restless legs at night - cramping
- Repeated tapping and hands/feet
- Uncontrollable sweating
- Cold hands and feet

Selenium
(Symptoms)

- Eczema
- Delayed wound healing
- Chronic urinary tract infections
- Increased susceptibility to yeast infections

Zinc
(Symptoms)

- Acne
- Staph infections
- Boils
- Ear infections - chronic
- Lack of smell/taste
- White spots on fingernails
- Blood sugar disturbances
- Sensitivity to light

- Growing pains
- Chapped lips

Digestive Enzymes
(Symptoms)

- Excessive gas
- White spots on fingernails
- Constipation
- Bowel pain
- Eczema

Essential Fatty Acid
(Symptoms)

- Sinus problems
- PMS
- Bleeding gums
- Brittle nails
- Hair loss
- Excess ear wax
- Cold hands and feet
- Dry, flaky skin

ELIMINATION

The following suggestions for eliminating certain foods (or substances) will allow the body to rest and heal itself. Attempt to eliminate the following:

- Junk food
- Sugar and sugar products (natural sugars are allowed)
- Milk and dairy products
- Food (and environmental substances) to which you suspect your child is allergic

In addition, try to:

- Avoid as many fried foods as possible.
- Keep fat intake to 20-30% of calories eaten
- Include flaxseed oil in the diet, e.g. over a salad (do not cook with flaxseed oil, as it becomes toxic when heated)
- Add chopped onions or garlic to the fat in the pan as it helps protect the fat from oxidation and produces even less toxic elements
- Sauté vegetables in broth or water for less toxicity
- Use butter rather than margarine, but use sparingly due to high fat content. Butter is more digestible than margarine and contains fewer chemicals and toxic products
- Eliminate many toxic cleaning products

Garlic
Stimulates the immune system, as well as serving as an antibacterial, antiviral and an antifungal element. It is a natural antibiotic and works actively to fight off infection. Use daily in cooking or as much as possible.
Onions
Assists the circulatory system and helps protect the liver.

EXCERPTS FROM DIALOGUE FOLLOWING WORKSHOPS

Q. You often refer to the children as "he". Do you not see girls?

A. While I do see girls, the majority of the children have been boys. Boys tend to be more hyper and therefore, are more of a problem. Girls, while they may be hyper, usually are more passive and are not labeled or identified as frequently. I use the term "he" just to simplify my responses.

Q. My husband is very much opposed to trying anything else as we've been everywhere and have had no success, however, we don't want our child on drugs. How can I encourage him to try this program?

A. In my experience mothers persist in their attempts to find a resolution more so than fathers. This has much to do with the way we generally deal with life situations as we integrate emotional and logical thinking. All of the fathers with whom I have worked have changed their minds during the program because the material is logical and is based on solid facts. They have become even more accepting when they witness the results.

Q. Most of your material seems to be directed towards helping children. What about adults.

A. Approximately 20% of my clients are adults. I teach the adults the cause of the disorder and the same drug-free program that will eliminate the disorder and put their lives back in order. I know how devastating and disruptive this disorder can be. My program can help you.

Q. My child listens to no one. How can we believe that he'll do as we say regarding your program?

A. If your child listens to no one, as you say, start with the 3rd part of the program, which is supplementation with vitamins and minerals. You will most likely notice your child becoming more agreeable. When this happens, share the other 2 parts of the program with him. If your child will not take his supplements, try giving 2 drops of Rescue Remedy™. This is an herbal tincture developed by Dr. Bach. Most health food stores sell this product. Many of my clients found than their child became compliant and it was easier to have them take their vitamins. Oils may be rubbed on the belly if he/she has a problem swallowing pills. Similarly, if vitamins present some difficulty, crush them and mix with food.

Q. My child has taken Ritalin™ and many other drugs over the course of several years. How long will it take until he can be off the drugs?

A. The drug manufacturer of Ritalin™ advises a daily drug holiday (after school to morning), along with a drug holiday on weekends. After your child has been on the program and is showing positive signs, start monitoring his behaviour more closely on Saturdays and Sundays. My clients have told me that when they noticed a change, they decided to try a drug-free Monday. If no complaints came from the school, they tried another day without the drugs. Other parents have tried cutting down the amount on a daily basis (i.e. instead of 2 pills, only 1-½). Over a period of a month or so, the child has successfully been weaned off the medication. Please consult with the health care professional who prescribed the medication.

Q. Once we begin the program, what can we expect to notice?

A. Parents tell me that the first signs are changes in behaviour. They appear to be calmer, more pleasant, less tired. Bedwetting and sleeping problems generally improve in a short period of time also.

Q. We have been to 8 medical doctors and they say that ADHD is a lifelong disorder.
A. This is true if one does not identify the underlying cause(s), however, the program I have developed, based on my research, uncovers the causes and teaches parents (and adults), what needs to be done in order to minimize or eliminate the symptoms.

Q. What kind of academic progress have the children on your program shown?
A. All of the children have done better once they have been on the program from 2 months to 1 year. Some children make 1-3 years progress in one school year. In fact, most of the children that I have worked with have shocked their teachers with their improvement.

Q. At what age have you started seeing children who have ADHD?
A. I have seen children as young as 3 years old. The parents of these children have been most concerned about their child's behaviour, have sought relief and have been told to put their child on Ritalin™ or one of the other prescribed drugs, e.g. Dexedrine™, Cylert™. Wanting a drug-free alternative, they have sought my help.

Q. My child has not been labeled ADHD, but we are having so many problems with him, and so is the school that we wonder if we have to wait for the labeling before we can help him?
A. Many parents know that there is a problem long before the school tells them it is so. Early intervention is preferred as more damage to the child's self-esteem can be avoided. In some cases, the child is just great at school and is never identified because he does not present the kind of problem that would justify the expense of the assessment. It has been my experience that these children wreak havoc at home.

Q. How easy will it be for me to have my child start the program?

A. It has been my experience that school-age children find the information empowering because they now understand just what has caused their problem and they gain insight into their behaviours and what causes them. This then allows them to shed the negative views about themselves. When you know what is causing the problem, you too will view your child differently and will be able to take positive action instead of being pulled into his/her chaos.

Q. My child has been on many antibiotics. What problems can this potentially cause?

A. Antibiotics can lead to the development of B vitamin deficiencies. Consult a naturopath, homeopath or your physician for the appropriate testing.

Q. My child is very stressed out about school. What does stress do to the body nutritionally?

A. Numerous experts will tell you that the amount of stress determines your nutritional requirements as stress readily depletes Vitamins C and B and Zinc.

Q. My son is 19 years old and is smoking and drinking alcohol. What effect will these habits have on his system?

A. Consumption of alcohol and smoking often induce nutritional deficiencies. Encourage your son to quit both. Definitely have him address the nutritional deficiencies by taking vitamins, etc..

Q. Since I have to eliminate sugar from my diet, and because I just love sweet-tasting things, can I use a sugar substitute?

A. Consuming refined sugar (even though bad for us) is not as bad as sugar substitutes which are produced from the waste of petrochemical products. Artificial sweeteners have been linked to many health problems. Many health professionals can provide suggestions for sugar substitutes.

Q. What preservatives should I be especially aware of?

A. Preservatives BHT and BHA destroy Vitamins A, C, and E. Eliminate processed food and substitute whole foods. Supplement the diet so that these vitamins are replenished.

Q. Dyes have been implicated in learning problems and hyperactivity since the 1970's. What do dyes do to the body?
A. Since food dyes inactivate Vitamin B_6, Folic acid and Vitamin C, nutritional deficiencies in these 3 vitamins can be induced.

Q. Does it matter what kind of vitamins I buy?
A. Yes. Synthetic food is always inferior to real food and so are synthetic vitamins inferior to whole food vitamins. Many companies today are making whole food supplements. Locate a source and buy those.

Q. My child really has difficulty around, or in chlorinated pools. His eyes become red, itchy and his nose runs. What can we do because he really loves to swim?
A. Chlorine is very difficult for some people to tolerate and these sensitive people demonstrate marked behavioural changes. Your child may even become aggressive, non-compliant, and very hyperactive when exposed to chlorine. If you live in an urban area, you and your family are getting daily doses of chlorine in your drinking and bathing water. Switch to distilled or filtered water, and purchase a charcoal filtered shower head to reduce exposure. Chlorine is known to inactivate thiamin and destroys Vitamins A, C, and E. Medical experts suggest giving extra A, C, and E before and after chlorine exposure to supply the body's needs, so if your child loves to swim, you may choose this option.

Q. My child and I really enjoy having desserts. With everything else we are eliminating, can we still have desserts? Are there sugar substitutes that I could cook with instead of sugar?
A. There is an excellent sugar substitute call Stevia™, which is 200 - 300 times sweeter than sugar. It produces no rise in blood sugar and doesn't feed yeast or micro-organisms. Check at your local health food store. If they don't carry it, ask them to order it for you.

SUGGESTED READING

Ash, J., Roberts, D., <u>Hyperactive Child (Beat Hyperactivity And Other Food Sensitivities With Quick And Easy Meals)</u>, Northamptonshire, England, Thorsons Publishing Ltd., 1990.

Balch, J.F., Balch, P.S., <u>Prescription For Nutritional Healing</u> New York; Avery Publishing Group Inc., 1990.

Bateson-Koch, <u>Allergies, Disease In Disguise</u>, Burnaby, British Columbia: Alive Books, 1994.

Beebe, G., <u>Toxic Carpet III</u>, Cincinnati, Ohio; 1991

Bell, Iris, <u>Clinical Ecology</u>, Bolinas, CA: common Knowledge Press, 1982.

Bland, Jeffrey, <u>Medical Applications Of Clinical Nutrition</u>, New Canaan, Connecticut: Keats Publishing, 1983.

Blume, K.A., <u>Air Pollution In The Schools And Its Effect On Our Children</u>, Chicago: Ecology Research Foundation, 1968.

Cohen, Sidney, <u>The Chemical Brain, The Neuro-Chemistry Of Addictive Disorder</u>, Irvine, CA: Care Institute, 1988.

Cott, A., Agel, J., <u>Dr. Cott's Help For Your Learning Disabled Child</u>, New York: Times Books, Random House, 1985.

Crook, William, G., <u>Allergy And How It Affects You And Your Child</u>, Jackson, TN: Professional Books, 1984.

Crook, W.G., <u>Solving The Puzzle Of Your Hard To Raise Child</u>, New York Random House, 1987.

Duffy, William, <u>Sugar Blues</u>, Radnor, Pennsylvania: Chilton Book Company, 1975.

Essman, W.G., ED., <u>Nutrients and Brain functioning</u>, New York: Karger Publishers, 1987.

Griggs, B., The Food Factor: An Account Of The Nutrition Revolution, Markham, Ontario: Penguin Books, 1988.

Healy, Jane, M., Endangered Minds, Why Children Don't Think And What We Can Do About It, New York: Simon & Schuster, 1990.

Hunter, Beatrice Trum, The Fact Book On Food Additives And Your Health, New Canaan, Connecticut: Keats Publishing Inc., 1990.

Kahan, B., Healthier Children: Professional Guidance For Parents In The Areas Of Nutrition, Environment And Behavior, New Canaan, Connecticut: Keats Publishing Inc., 1990.

Krohn, J., The Whole Way To Allergy Relief And Prevention, Vancouver, British Columbia: Hartley and Marks Ltd., 1991.

Melvill, A., Cured To Death: The Effects Of Prescription Drugs, New York: Steen and Day, 1982.

Randolph, T.G., An Alternative Approach To Allergies, New York: Harper and Row, 1989.

Rapp, D.J., The Impossible Child, Buffalo: Practical Allergy Foundation, 1989.

Rapp, D.J., Allergies And Your Family, Buffalo: Practical Allergy Foundation, 1980.

Schroeder, Henry, A., The Poisons Around Us: Toxic Metals In Food, Air And Water, Bloomington: Indiana University Press, 1974.

Weissman, J.D., M.D., Choose To Live - A Ten Point, Ten Week Program For Eliminating The Environmental Toxins That Threaten Your Health, New York: Penguin Books, 1989.

Williams, Roger, Biochemical Individuality, Austin, Texas: University of Texas Press, 1979.

Wunderlich, R.C., Allergy, Brains And Children Coping, St. Petersburg, Florida: Johnny Reads, 1973.

If you do not read anything else, you owe it to yourself to read Dr. Frank Oski's book entitled Don't Drink Your Milk. Dr. Oski is a medical doctor and at the time of writing his book was the Director, Department of Pediatrics, Johns Hopkins University School of Medicine, and Physician-in-Chief, the Johns Hopkins Children's Center. His book was first published in 1977, and its ninth edition was published in 1992.

RECAP

**It is advisable to consult a health care professional prior to
beginning the program**

1. Review the contents of this book and discuss the program ideas
   with family members.
2. Buy distilled water, or an alternate source, other than tap water.
   Start replacing soda pop, juice and milk with water, so that the
   child/adult is consuming 6 - 8 glasses of water per day. Limit the
   amount of juice because of its sugar content. Please note that
   during this initial period, more frequent bathroom trips will be
   unavoidable. Once the body adjusts to using water, the number of
   visits will be reduced.
3. Eliminate cow's milk and all dairy products. You may substitute
   goat's milk, goat cheese, or other cheese products from the Health
   Food Store (e.g. tofu products). Rice and Soya milk are also good
   alternatives. Pasteurization has killed all enzymes in milk and its
   products, making it difficult to digest. If you cannot eliminate milk
   completely at first, try to mix rice or Soya milk with cow's milk.
   Use ¾ of a cup of cow's milk and ¼ of a cup of the other; then
   ½ cup of cow's milk and ½ cup of the other, until you gradually
   eliminate cow's milk altogether.
4. Visit your local health food store and purchase products listed. If
   you cannot afford to purchase all of the products as once, start by
   purchasing the plant enzymes, followed by the Essential Fatty Acids
   and then, multiple vitamins and minerals. If you are purchasing

whole food vitamins, follow the regime suggested by the distributor. Plant enzymes are also key supplements in whole food vitamins.

5. Start a daily journal in which you record symptoms noted, food consumed, and both physical and behavioural changes that occur. Not all changes are readily apparent; some changes creep up on you. Physical symptoms will wane first. Behaviour will improve next and the ability to learn and do, will be the last area to show improvement. It is a good idea to frequently review the questionnaire at the beginning of the workbook so you can see the improvements being made.

6. Identify 5 favourite foods of your child or yourself, as these are most likely to be the cause of chronic health problems. Look for reactions to the most frequently eaten foods and write in your journal any physical, behavioural, and cognitive observations after ingesting these foods. Start eliminating these foods one by one. As discussed in the Withdrawal Section, you may experience some discomfort when eliminating these foods, but just remember your body is trying to get back into balance.

7. Be patient and stay as close to the program as possible. Some changes will be noticeable within the 1st - 4th weeks, although changes may take longer for some. Reflect on how long you or your child has shown symptoms and be realistic in your expectations. Some clients have had a completely "different" child in 2 months, while other children have taken 6 months to a year to show such dramatic improvement.

8. Start an exercise program. It helps the body to detoxify. Keep it simple and initially aim for 30-minute duration, 3 times a week. Any form of physical activity is suitable but it is a must! Try to encourage a family walk before or after dinner.

Inspire Others

In the fall of 1999 I was again working in a school environment and was asked to observe a grade 3 student as the teacher was concerned about her level of skills. As this was a new placement for me I reviewed the girl's school records prior to visiting the classroom. After a short time I noticed the extent of eczema affecting the girl's exposed skin. In speaking with her she told me how much her body hurt and how uncomfortable she was most days. Following this meeting I called her mother and asked her to come and meet with me at the school. During this meeting we discussed her daughter's medical history, medication and reviewed her academic progress and acquisition of skills. I explained my research and subsequent program and inquired whether she would like to try this approach. After one week she returned to the school ready to try this approach. By Christmas the girl showed much improvement in eczema outbreaks, was sleeping better, had more energy and the teacher reported that the girl was more attentive and was showing some academic gains. By June she was functioning at a midgrade 3 level. We transferred her to grade 4 and throughout this year she achieved 1 year and 6 months progress, thereby closing the academic gap.

I followed her progress throughout elementary school and periodically throughout high school. Her mother called me with updates. In grade 12 she was chosen valedictorian for her graduating class and doing very well. Eczema flare-ups were infrequent and only appeared when she was very tired, stressed or had not been following a good diet.

I was again reminded of how we all can teach and help one another as it was one of my previous clients who first alerted me to the effect of nutrient therapy in dealing with eczema. Her child was diagnosed with ADHD, had severe eczema, was on medication and was lagging academically. After attending one of my workshops and then following the program the mother reported that her daughter's eczema was showing significant improvement. This had not previously happened despite years of dermatological treatments. This revelation has been shared with, and has helped, many others over the years. Now let your insights help others.

www.ingramcontent.com/pod-product-compliance
Lightning Source LLC
Chambersburg PA
CBHW020301290526
45784CB00003B/1321